The

Artifice

Of

Infinity

The Artifice Of Infinity

J. Gardner Hodder

Black Iris Press
Toronto

The Artifice of Infinity.

For information contact **Black Iris Press**,
77 King Street West, Suite 1900, Box 40,
Royal Trust Tower, Toronto-Dominion Centre,
Toronto, Canada M5K 1B7
Tel: (416) 601-1312 Fax: (416) 947-0909

First Printing 1993
Cover Art and Design: Symbols, Toronto
Back Cover Photo: Kimberly Pettit
Printed on Recyled, Acid-free Paper
Printed and Bound in Canada

Canadian Cataloguing in Publication Data

Hodder, J. Gardner (James Gardner), 1955-
The artifice of infinity

Written in blank verse.
ISBN 0-9696580-0-1

I. Title

PS8565.043A8 1993 C811'.54 C92-095695-5
PR9199.3.H63A8 1993

Table of Contents

Acknowledgements

I would like to acknowledge the kind assistance and encouragement of Tamara Crispin, Bois Wilson, Randolph Joyce and Robert Curtin.

J. G. H.

To my wife, Elizabeth

Author's Preface

From Homer to Pratt, narrative verse has concerned itself with the enhancement of history and culture through established mythologies. The modern imagination, however, usually prefers to create its own myths for its own purposes.

For this, the premise of science fiction provides a relatively blank canvas. Writing the history of an imagined future, rather than of the actual past, the mythmaker may explore human nature with fewer restrictions. As I hope will be apparent in the pages that follow, narrative verse—with its own panoply of special effects—is quite compatible with speculation of this kind.

I am indebted to British physicist Stephen Hawking for recently popularizing the concepts of event horizons and singularities. I had completed in 1987 a plot outline for *The Artifice of Infinity*. When Dr. Hawking's book, *A Brief History of Time*, appeared the following year, I rejoiced, as a non-scientist, to obtain so much comprehensible theoretical assistance. I was also relieved to learn that the main "scientific fiction" of *The Artifice*—namely, physical causation extending into and then out of a black hole—was, according to the scientists, indeed fiction.

Fortunately, up to the date of publication, this view has remained unchanged.

J. Gardner Hodder
December, 1992
Toronto

The Arrival

Chapter 1

The Arrival

Here is a story which, by being told,
ensures that its events may keep their force,
in face of all the limits, or the
boundlessness, of space, or any flux of time.
Give thought in common on that day when it
began, a point of time and space condensed
beyond all measure, all still to unfold.

The crystal caves, around the mountain's crest,
above the lesser peaks whose crowded stony
faces pressed from every side, were that day
so quiet. The Planet of the Silver Streams,
so named for shining waters from those hills,
lay bathed in clotted puffs of silver cloud;
and warmed beneath its double orange suns,

it turned, as slow as if there were no time,
or if there were, then time was very slow.
    Twelve caves above the cloud, all broad across
and ranged about the craggy summit's brow,
each filled with massive gems—a cubic yard
were some—in brimming indentations
cupped twelve portions of deluging sun,
which overflowed and spilled their light, from facets
full of glare, in jets of golden force
that hissed through wandering wisps of smoky haze
and left the atmosphere, sending then their
blinding greeting to the planet's twenty moons.
    This world came into being, as does art,
with brushstrokes leaving rock and sky and light.
Its silver waters, like an inlaid metal
netting, stretched between the shores of molten
silver seas. Its hills, like woven beads
of sun baked clay, made casual adornment
in between the painted plains. The hands
of careful planning made this world a lasting
monument to Higher Species' Craft,
of all three Species—Tersai, Human, Kowd.
Thus this world spun, an orbiting display
of what the Higher Species could create,
and decorate, and beautify as worlds
which they designed and set throughout all space.
    The mountain's crystals' purpose was to give
all starbeams place to find their resting mark

when, by transmission to the starbeams' reach,
the Higher Species spanned galactic waste.
The caves were poised to bring the beams to rest,
to bend the lightspeed starbeams from their slow
and lonely piercing of the empty void,
and, after eons of their travel's sleep,
to welcome new arrivals, and their news.
These caves were called the Caves of Starbeams' Rest.

Within the mountain, at the caves' controls,
a pador sat and watched the many screens
that flickered, all, with signals from afar.
The signals came from many foreign worlds
and shared new thoughts, which, when arrived, were old.

This animal, a pador quite well trained,
was content to sit, day upon long day,
fine-tuning for the constant in-transmission
of which so little he could understand—
until, that day, one screen made all things change;
and to his feet the wide-eyed pador rose
and was unsteady, seeing words appear
that, straining his capacity to read,
revealed to him there soon would be, at hand,
three sets of signals of a starbeam's force
which, recomposed, bring visitors to life;
and not enough that these would be the first
arrivals in ten thousand Centrayears,
the first to visit since, so long ago,
the Planet of the Silver Streams was made

and hung in furthest murky space to shine;
and not enough these starbeams took their source
upon the Planet Centra's broad plateau;
it also seemed—the pador puzzled here—
this was importance with no precedent at all.

Faster than the silver drops of rivers
flowed and frothed downhill, the pador pressed his
paws to winding flowered paths that tumbled,
downward, to the valley and to whom he
must now go: Bal Planetlord, the sovereign
ruler of that world of silver streams.

This planetlord, a Tersai calm and kind,
performed his lordly duties on that world
as they from time to time arose: sometimes
to help the padors when the farmland needed
rain, or to preside when, every several
hundred Centrayears, all Beings gathered when
the Oracle had uttered words and made
pronouncement, or, sometimes, more rarely, to
convene the planet's Wisest Ones to hear
suggestions or petitions to increase
the common good—or on that day to greet
the pador's frenzied pounding on his door.

It took some time for this so strange hard noise
to break the soft and misty trance that lay
about the planetlord and his fair wife,
good Olsta, pure and bright, and at that time
so tender to his touch, so eager were

they both to pass the afternoon in love,
reclining naked with no pause for breath
until they rose to greet the breathless pador.
"With such regret, sweet Olsta, must I go,"
Bal Planetlord soon said, "for even though
the pador's words are hard to understand,
he strains to say such things that if I were
ten trillion Centrayears a planetlord,
I might not have such reason to depart
from you and from our tender day in bed."
"You know so well," his wife said in reply,
"that if the world outside should end, and plunge
into our suns, I would not care, so long
as I had you, this room, and time for love—
but now be gone, straight to the mountain's top;
and I will call around and gather here
those of the Tersai, Humans and the sexless
Kowd who, from our planet, should be here
to greet and welcome those from Centra come."
With kisses, then, less lingered than they wished,
they parted to this sudden duty's call,
he through the quiet town, along the marble
walks through cooling purple ferns so common
to that world. His emotion was concern.
He could have no fear, nor could he feel
the tinge of any apprehension from
the news the pador brought. All reasons for
unpleasantness of thought, actual or

perceived, had been, in distant and
forgotten ages past, long since abolished.
None of the Higher Species had for eons
tasted pain, or death, or hunger, war or grief,
and had not, since the padors could be trained,
done work or any task beyond the scope
of inclination's power to persuade.

The Planetlord sped up the steep incline
toward the sun-soaked Caves of Starbeams' Rest;
and just as it had been his humble way,
and sense of duty's call, that were the reasons
he was asked, so many Centrayears ago,
to take the mantle of the Planetlord,
his duty also pressed him to the cavern
floor, with arms outstretched before the
reassembling forms, which having glanced along
a hundred galaxies, now funnelled through
the Crafting of the caves; and swathed in light,
there came, from energy to substance, three,
three souls from Centra with no notice come,
three Beings from the Great and Universal Source.

Upon the polished gleaming platforms, cut
from clearest slabs of diamond, the trio
stood reflected in the perfect gemstone
surfaces. By their garb and its design,
Bal Planetlord saw here was presence of
the highest and unequalled rank: three envoys
of the solemn Overlords themselves;

and each one bore the emblems of Attendants
of the Source. One was Human, one Kowd,
and one was Tersai, like himself, who spoke:
"Arise, and take our hands, O Planetlord.
In joy we have arrived. I am I La,
first of this equal three whom you behold
and who come here directly at the Overlords'
request. The Human female with me is
the beautiful Ito; and Ti Rathu,
true to the way of Kowd, would rather have
me speak for it—and so for it, and us,
I give you greeting in the Centran way."
He gave Bal Planetlord a kiss and then
deferred to Ito, who spoke, "Our purpose here
is grave, and do not wonder that we come
so far." She smiled a practiced, calming smile.
"You, yourself, as planetlord, know well
that to control the weather overhead
you must apply your Craft in distant parts—
for distance is nearby in its effect—
and you, to bring the rain to slake the growth
that is your food, must coax the scattered cloud
from pole to pole. Thus we are come today
from Centra, Great and Universal Source,
to find here, at the limit of deep space,
the answer to an urgent Centran need."
Ti Rathu, the Kowd, was immobile;
for as the Kowd are species without limbs

and without eyes, it could not see nor move;
and true to type, it chose to say no word
and to preoccupy itself with thought.

Bal Planetlord found strength to overcome
his awe and said, in formal reverence, thus:
"O fellow Tersai, lady Human, Kowd,
I La, Ito and silent Ti Rathu,
ambassadors of that exalted world,
Centra, great fulcrum of the government
of space—of what is known, and of what can
be known—accept from me and feel within
your hearts, and know within your noble minds,
ten thousand welcomes for each star you passed
along the way, from Centra to this world,
this little known, less populated place
of rivulets of dancing silver light.
Whatever help there is in my resource,
you three shall surely have. Come now with me,
and I shall be your guide to take you from
this mountain's core, where pressed reflections bend
all light and give distortion to the starbeam's
recent noble gifts, you worthy three.
Now shield your eyes against the solar blast
which fiercely strikes this place of silver streams,
and we shall go to where you all may rest."

The Tersais both, I La and Planetlord,
leaned forward, out of habit, to lift
the limbless, sightless Kowd. This was long

customary use of great untiring Tersai
strength, a thousand times that of the Human
and infinitely beyond that of the Kowd,
whose greater force lay in the wisdom of
their long considered words. Thus they started
down in steps of solemn, measured march,
descending townward through the purple leaves,
where, to three huts of calm and soft repose,
the guests were taken to collect their thoughts
before they met the evening's banquet crowd.

Alone within their humble thatched retreat,
sweet Olsta took her mate in soft embrace
and whispered to him thus: "Good Planetlord,
I have sent word to all the far extremes;
and there will be collected here, tonight,
as many of the foremost of our world
as this short notice will permit; but know
that this great joy, in being honored thus,
in having here such noble visitors,
is equalled, no, exceeded, by the great
urgency of my love; and please, you must,
for yet there is some time before the feast,
take me and show me by your gentle touch
some new expression of your endless love;
for though there is all time for us to learn
unending lessons of what joins our hearts,
I cannot learn too quickly, and quickly,

now, before, you see, my words give way to breath:
come share with me the moistness of my mood."

With eyes half-closed and hands exploring down
his shoulders to his muscled Tersai waist,
she nodded to the servant padors that
they quickly leave the room; yet Bal drew back
and said, "O splendid, sweetest Olsta, well
I know and cherish mutual desire,
which, in the more than million Centrayears
since you and I have wed, gives us such joy,
and which, but moments after we have made
the sweetest love there is, begins again
to stir us to our rhythmic deep embrace;
but, hear me, how my senses, and my thought,
are overcome with what these Centran Beings
say—explain it, I cannot. Some feeling
stirs that I have never felt. No. I say
no more." He turned and quickly dressed himself
in rich green robes of silk, for formal feast,
and left a puzzled Olsta to her thoughts.

When all had eaten, late that crowded night,
and rituals of welcome were complete,
the banquet hall grew still, all charged with
expectation from the unexpected guests,
as through the vaulted windows blew cool
evening breezes, that on the ceiling scattered
dotted candlelight, reflected from
the shifting curtains spun of silver thread.

A deeply learned Kowd, who had not spoken
in twelve thousand years, spoke from its place:
"Beings of the Planet of the Silver Streams,
those who are here, or by transmission present,
give now your listening selves to all grave words
of these three Centran high ambassadors."

Ito stood and thus addressed the many:
"The Council of the Overlords at Centra
sends its greeting. We three give thanks for all
the welcomes you have shown us in this
distant place, this marvel of a world of
liquid light. The Oracle, which though confined
to Centra governs every being in
all space, has sent us here to one sure goal:
to find among you here, and take with us,
a certain special Aliadni who,
in the judgment of your Wisest Ones,
is, on this planet, most profoundly wise
and fully learned in the Way of Life,
which is your planet's special Craft and lore.
You must not ask the reason for this quest.
The great and mysterious Oracle,
sometimes, requires us to give assistance
doing deeds of which we only know
they must be done. As we, and you, obey
in this, the Planet Centra rules all space."

At that, the hall erupted in applause
and wild cheers, for so they loved to hear

the all-assuring dictum of the Centran
rule. That night the silver planet pulsed
with pride for having been brought into play
of what concerned all space. Some said that Bal
should shortly make a pador holiday
so that the planet's slaving beasts might know,
in respite from the workshops and the fields,
the honor which had come; and to others,
who dwelled upon the planet's circling moons,
it seemed the world had quickened in its turning.

Next day, the planet's Wisest Ones conferred;
and, since Olsta ranked among their number,
she was not home when Ito came to call,
or when that Centran envoy nestled her
lithe form among the piled cushions, smiled,
and spoke to the awestruck planetlord, thus:

"I saw today, before the sky grew light,
the delta at your eastern shore, where
coursing through the sand and silt of purest gold,
the silver river greets the silver sea;
and there I watched this planet's fabled dawn,
the lifting up of your two orange stars,
which, at the moment when they crossed the sharp
horizon's mirrored edge, by sheer brilliance
blurred distinction of the sky and of the
calm reflecting sea—thus there were four suns,
and whitest sky began, beneath my feet,
at what had been, by night, the water's edge.

"All Beings of this planet take delight
in the perfection, and the beauty, of
this scene; but, Bal Planetlord, consider
how the artful framers of this fair world,
to make the ocean daybreak such a sight,
relied upon illusion of the eyes,
and how the pleasure of your senses is
increased, not by what is, but by what seems."

"I know," said Bal, "that when the Oracle
confirmed the edict of the Overlords
that this bright world be built, here, at the limit
where the pioneers of space have gone,
the architects applied all finest Craft.
They put two model planets—this, and our
neighbor planet, Attatrul—in orbit
of the double suns; and they formed beauty
worth long years of travel through the empty
reach of space. This world of silver streams
became a polished glory cast in metal,
rock and light; and Attatrul was then a
garden planet, the greenest of all—
but what seemed then would be two places much
desired, in fact, have been near vacant,
completed, as they were, just at the time
the Leaves of Love, at Centra, came to bloom.
There then commenced a new Great Age of Love,
eclipsing this great canvas, hung in space."

"You miss my point," said Ito. "I will tell
you what I mean. Your Wisest Ones choose now
who should return to Centra with us three.
In fact there is no choice. The Oracle
wants you, and only you, Bal Planetlord;
and for good reasons which I can't explain,
the Oracle demands that you now seem
to be the choice of your assembled wise.
You must not think of what you leave behind,
but rather, go prepare yourself to leave;
and quickly we shall go, once we have learned,
from Olsta here, your wisdom's nominee."

Just then returning, Olsta saw Bal's face
and said, "I cannot think what passes through
your mind, my planetlord, but never have
I seen you look so at a loss for words—
and this in presence of our noble guest—
but here, in this sealed scroll is marked the name
of whom the Wisest Ones have picked to go:
you first shall know our secret ballot's fruit."

"There is so much I do not understand,"
said Bal, taking in his trembling hand the scroll,
"and you, good Olsta, will not know, as surely
I do not, how any Being's speech
may, with intent, speak other than the truth—
I can't recall the ancient word for speaking
what's not true—but we must now, on highest
order of the Great and Universal Source,

defend appearance from the truth we know,
the truth, which, when you counted wisdom's vote,
you wrote within the seal which now I break,
and which inside reveals the name of Tol,
a Human male, who lives secluded in
our most remote antarctic frigid South.
Destroy this scroll. Say that I was chosen.
Then, for however many million years
that I am gone, assume the governance
of this, the lovely planet we call home."

The Centran envoys left, and with them, Bal;
and while the planet's beings, Tersai, Kowd
and Human, could assume the suddenness
of leaving was in answer to some great
urgency, not one was able to resolve
the puzzle of fair Olsta, calm and wise,
who by some force unknown was rendered mute.

The Table

Chapter 2

The Table

The waters lapped against the dull gray cliffs;
and, in among them, rocked great slabs of ice
like crowded ships of chrome in rolling seas
of mercury. Above, in frosty, milk-white skies,
loud, clapping flocks of reptile birds
flew searching down the savage coast, among
its weathered rocks, to find and eat the hairless
rodents darting there, who unlike the
Higher Species knew fear, and feared their death.

Behind the cliffs, and like a frosted mirror
stretching out of sight, lay shimmering plains
of silver snow, unbroken but for peaks
created by volcanoes' angry force.
In these, deep raging heat ignited still
their clustered smoking cones in noise and fire;

and for some miles among these towering hills,
except for blackened places of the lava's
recent touch, the lush and purple fronds
of densest growth took root, in steaming soil,
and marked the bounds of an oasis from
the bitter cold. While there had been no plan,
by framers of that world, for anyone
to live in this remote, antarctic place,
Tol, the Aliadni, kept here his home,
a two-room hut of bark and twisted straw.
Next to it was another where his
padors took their rest. This gentle Human here
kept long strange refuge in his thoughts, his books,
and in the warbling music of his flute.

Above the valley's richness, and its life,
the moistness of its breezes turned to fog;
and caught by dagger blasts of icy air,
it changed again to thick white streams of cloud,
so dense, sometimes, they blotted out the suns
in racing layers, carpeting the ground
in shadow, wreathing round the rumbling peaks,
darkening the slanted summer daylight
into gloom, and, when all the light was gone,
reminding Tol of what concealed the
mysteries that lay as memory, within,
and which obscured the feelings and the thoughts
he longed and dreamed to think and feel again.

Approaching on the frigid plains of snow,
there came one day a single wooden sled.
It slipped along on pointed metal skis
and sped through bitter winds and blinding glare,
propelled by sweating padors' racing feet,
until it reached the shadows at the limit
of the snow. Just there the padors stopped;
and stepping from the sled inside the warm
and foggy gloom, a bright-eyed Tersai named
Asara cupped her hands to shout for Tol;
and casting off the furs which kept her warm,
she sent a pador running to announce
she had arrived. She stood a moment thinking
how she loved this lonely hermit Tol,
and with what soft, adoring, tender passion
he loved her, and had for centuries
so loved, although he strained her patience by
refusing her the pleasures of his bed.

With loping strides as come from Tersai strength,
she made her way along the valley floor
to find him, lest her pador be delayed;
and passing soon the pador who had stopped
to peer, confused, inside the empty huts,
she paced through pillowed clouds of heavy fog
until she came, breathless, to sloping mounds
which rose between two great volcanic cones,
one live, one dormant. Upon a shelf of stone
which bridged the mountains' sides, she saw her Tol.

He stood before a broad and boiling pool,
which, on one side, was fed by tinselled streams
unravelling down the quiet mountain's side,
but from the thundering side, with smoke and heat,
was made alive with hissing liquid fire
that sent the water skyward, powered both
by crimson lava and by whistling jets
of upward drafting air. With arms outstretched,
and legs apart, not seeing Asara,
Tol bellowed to the elemental force:
"Now purge me of what is, and what will be,
and all that is the past that I recall.
Now let me pierce the void of cancelled thought
and bridge the unpassed waters raging round
the islands of an Aliadni's dreams!"

As if in answer, massive scalding sheets
of water downward poured upon his taut,
unmoving form; and although, as Human,
Tol could feel no pain, nor suffer any
hurt, or even know what pain could be,
he somehow sensed that some great meaning lay
in how his body made its self-repair.

"Tol, see who's here, and come into my arms,"
Asara spoke, and shook him from his thoughts.
She climbed the rocks, in tears, and ran to him;
and Tol fell to his knees. He clasped her waist;
and as she smoothed his hair and held him close,
they swore a hundred sweet and tender vows

of how so much each had the other missed,
and longed for, dreamed of, and lived a lesser
life without the strong, sure comforts of their love.
These two embraced until completely drenched
from hot cascading water and their tears.

"My good Tol," said soft Asara, later,
as they ate, "the filtered light of our bright
planet's many moons, through your small windows,
makes a dance of colors on your floor
as if to call your exile to its end.
They beckon you to join a normal life,
outside, beyond this lonely cell of straw,
far from this freak, antarctic hothouse place
of isolation. In all directions
northward, the Higher Species of this world
live out the calm and measured harmony
of lives entwined in love. Then, why not you?
Have you not tasted of the Leaves of Love
and journeyed, half across the universe,
to join, by eating of that plant, the souls
of tens of trillions—Tersai, Human, Kowd—
who, as pilgrims to the Planet Centra,
have joined each other in the bond of Love?

"Why not return, up north, to where the streams
of silver flow, and where our lives could pass
in gentle sports, amusing games, and walks
through purple woods? Replace lonely boredom
with the joys of village life, with days of

painting, sculpting, staging silly plays,
or dreaming under shady ferns relaxed
by liquored tea, or chatting happy hours
away with neighbors in the park, or in
the evening singing, dancing, feasting full.
Learn how others play the flute. Bring your books,
and tell to others what you've learned.
Find relaxation in the pleasant weariness
of sports, and find in others context for
your thought; and you could be exploring
other pleasures of a life in love with me."

Tol shook his head, and smiled at her, and said,
"A bird within a flock hears but his friends.
When centuries ago I lived among
my fellow kind, I set myself a task
to learn what lies beyond our purposes
in life, and whether any goal exists
beyond the high and universal doctrines
taught of love, and being all in love,
and whether there, all action, striving, thought
begin and end. Around me, every time
I posed my quest, the Humans and the Tersai
said, 'How plainly it is so: all is love';
and never was a Kowd inclined to speak,
except for one: Kowd Parinmawada,
who, learned in the history of space,
considered my unanswered thoughts. It said
I should direct my listening to silence;

and this was all it said. Then, as you know, I
took great slabs of crystal rock, and fashioned,
with aid of ancient doctrine, lore and Craft,
a Table to receive the mystery
of the Oracle, to bring directly
to this planet emanations of the
Great and Universal Source, and, with this,
to shatter all the bonds that bind my thought.

"It was ready. I was fully prepared.
But on the day to link my finite mind
to knowledge without bound, the Planetlord,
and several of the Wisest Ones, approached
and told me this ambition was too great—
and that the proper governance of space
required that there be one access to
the Oracle, and only one, and that
I might disturb the smooth concentric flow,
from Centra, of edicts, plans and orders,
which at the pace of light infuse all space
and guide the Higher Species and their worlds.

"At first I thought I might defy this plea
and follow my inquiry to its end;
and this might have been, but for fair Olsta,
spouse of Bal Planetlord and deepest friend
of yours, who slyly crossed your path with mine;
and all my turmoil ceased in your caress,
your glowing beauty, gentle speech, your love,
and, most of all, your steady patience with

what neither you nor I can understand:
the restless deep impulsion of my thoughts.
I balance on a prism of desire—
one facet: to defy my sovereign lord
and go in search, alone, of distant truths;
or then another: to unleash with you
uncounted nights and days of passion's touch.
The first is wrong; the other would defer
forever my great project of the mind.
There but remains the crystal's bottom side—
to listen to Parinmawada's words
and to retreat to wordlessness down here."
    Asara pressed her lips into a line,
and then she stepped away from where they ate.
In half a moment's deft unbuttoning,
she stepped out of her garments, facing Tol.
Soft shadows from the candlelight flickered on
her firm and gently rounded nakedness;
and as he watched, she ran her fingers down
the perfect contours of her perfect form.
    "These breasts and hips and thighs," Asara said,
"have been too long denied the press of love;
and I have yearned too much for your real love,
a love which does, and not just merely says,
a love for every day, not now and then,
a love that lives with me and not the wild.
I know you have a project to pursue
and that you live to find the words that link

the fragments of an Aliadni's past—
and other things I better sense than say.
Consider now this dreary, lonely place,
and fix your eyes on what your life rejects.
Come take me in your arms, and to your bed,
and learn, at last, how oneness of ourselves
will fill your needs, and fuel, not foil, your dreams."

Tol went to her and took her in his arms.
He felt her warmth and her slow moving form
against him; once again, he felt desire
eclipsing every other thought and plan;
but making now no effort to resist,
he slowly drew toward her parted lips.
They kissed. They felt themselves, so long restrained,
relax, at last, for playing out their dreams;
but this building passion was suspended by
a pador's urgent knocking at the door.

Asara turned, wide-eyed, toward the sound;
but close behind her, Tol stretched out his arms
and drew her close, exploring both her breasts.
He whispered through the softness of her hair,
"Twin soul, true love, eternal light for me,
think now of what importance waits outside
that door; and tell me that your thoughts match mine,
that nothing, though this planet burst apart,
should break up now those things that we would join:
our hungered bodies, pulsing to make love
and to ascend the summit of deep want."

With no more words or thoughts of what compelled
the pador to continue with his noise,
they hurried to the cushions of Tol's sleep.
Once there, amid long kisses of relief,
one for each day that they had been apart,
they found a rhythm, searching and slow,
which, he in her, and she around him, built
steadily toward the wild taut release that,
when it came, left them hurtling downward
off a precipice of frantic, clutching love,
with breathing almost panicked and dizziness
that shrouded their descent to normal pulse
amid deep moans of paroxysmic force;
and at last they rested, all altitudes
explored, their love declared, and passion spent.
Asara dressed, and Tol went to the door.
The pador, one of hers, explained that,
with the others, he had watched the telescreen
Asara brought upon the baggaged sled;
and he had learned Bal Planetlord had gone
and, with the Centran envoys, shot through space,
asleep for all the years the journey took
to Centra. Hastened then by strange concern,
Tol and Asara went and stood before
the screen, whose glow lit up the padors' hut
with northern news. Their puzzlement was made
acute as much by Planetlord's departure,
abrupt and unexplained, as by the fact

and mystery that Olsta could not speak.
Yet these events, for Tol, bore sudden meaning,
as he declared with eyes alight and flashing:
"I sense, by unknown faculties beyond
the normal five, that these strange things direct
me now towards the Source, towards the Centran
world and all the wisdom it contains.
The fruits of my long meditation here,
here at the limit's limit of all space,
may now, in this, their application find.
Among my books, one ancient tome describes
a quaint device known as a lock and key.
This thing was used, it seems—before the ways
which the great Second Abolition brought—
to prevent invasions unpermitted
within spaces which the lock controlled.
This ban on curiosity, I suppose,
depended on uniqueness of the fit—
the key into the lock. The holder of
the key controlled the space. I think I have
the means to form the key that will unbind
these mysteries, though how, I hardly know.
Although I but diffusely feel this fact,
I am prepared to dream the starbeam's sleep
and follow fate to try all locks at Centra.
For love, for us, to make our lives complete,
will you, Asara, join me in this quest?"

"If I could be a lock," she then replied,
you surely are the key. To you my life,
my body, dreams and hopes are never closed;
but, even as I once assisted in
dissuading you from seeking direct linkage
with the Great and Universal Source,
my Tersai caution and my deep concern
now tell me you should dare that bold attempt.
Apply your Craft and all your knowledge of
the Way of Life, and seek the Source from here."
She made Tol's thoughts fall inward on
themselves, as his returning gaze took back silence
from her eyes. Outside, volcanic rumbling
shocked the quiet air and startled into flight
uncounted waves of panicked, dark-scaled wings.
Both the suns, now rising, began to shine
between the twisted blankets of the
misty gloom. Soon, pausing only long enough
to seal their great resolve, and greater love,
with one last blissful kiss, Tol and Asara
herded all the padors to a nearby cave,
where Tol had stored the makings of his
forbidden Craft—those deftly chiselled crystal
forms, which, before the suns had hurdled noon,
stood interlocked and seamless against the
changing sky, with vaulting turrets shooting
down, to one vast Table, all their castled light.

In front of this square pool of sparkling fire,
Tol stood and shut his eyes and raised his voice,
intoning words as fit his mystic Craft.
Some words he only felt and did not
understand; and as his measured phrases
tumbled ever faster from his lips, the wind
changed all around and blew the sky all clear,
bathing him, Asara and the huddled
padors in one wide band of unbroken
double-shadowed light, which, cascading down
upon the angled crystal facets of
this so strange machine of light, exploded
on the Table before Tol. As he spoke,
bright pulsing patterns soon took shape and flashed
in answer to his every word, and then
nearby volcanic rumbling took this pace
until the words and sound and light were one.
At this, Tol knew that from across the farthest
span of jet-black space he stood in presence,
finally, of the only one true Source.

"Now ask!" Asara prompted, sensing what
took place. Yet before his several questions
reached Tol's tongue, a mighty voice of stern, sharp tones
was heard, or rather thought; for without noise
it sounded sense directly in their skulls.

Thus it spoke: "*Silence, Tol, and hear the Source.*
Go quickly now to Planet Attatrul.
Know that the Petition is denied."

As if stricken by this voice of thunder,
or, like Tol, confused by so much unexplained,
the towered structures of his long worked Craft
began to sway, then crack; and then they fell
into a crashing heap of gemstone dust and rubble.
After several minutes of unshaking
both their minds from what occurred, these two
lovers wondered at the silence, and the rain.

The Crater

Chapter 3

The Crater

Consciousness flickered out of nothingness
as, from the starbeam's flow, Tol slowly was
released. Assembling from the random void
from world to world that in one hour's pulse
the beam had shot, his senses, still half dreaming,
staggered all around a melting image
of Asara. This, from stellar sleep
and fitful restlessness to be awake,
became a phantom, and a ghost, and would
have seemed, but for the fact that he could know
no fear, a nightmare that their love would end.

With what seemed noiseless sounds of crackling
through his recongealing brain, the subatomic
makings of his firmer self took shape.
From deep within a bent and jagged flash,

what had been nothing now arrived, as Tol,
on Attatrul, his brief transmission's end.
Through blank half-lidded eyes, he saw a small
and smiling pador focus into life.
"So welcome, Tol," the nodding creature said
and helped him down, across the wooden floor;
and wondering how the pador knew his name,
so unexpected, unannounced was he,
Tol followed as the friendly beast then showed
him to the vast and open door of the
transmission hut, an opening vaulted skyward
with the knotted gnarls of the planet's
rock-hard amber wood. Outside, there stretched to
the horizon's clouded edge, the thick and
leafy treetops weaving on that world its
second surface, a life two hundred feet
above the mossed and darkly shaded ground.
The colors made, on that suspended plane,
a yellow-flowered tapestry of green.

Behind the pador's bobbing form, Tol stepped
along the foot-worn way. It twisted through
thick, languid banks of hot and humid haze
made even heavier by golden sprays
of pollen. He thought how little did he
know of what design the future drew for him,
or why he was on Attatrul, or where
this pador was so keen to lead. A shift
of wind pressed down the trembling petals at

his feet and made them flutter. Some clouds came,
and joined, and darkened, and dropping jagged
knives of white-hot molten light, cracked the sudden
gloom in fitted plates, back-lit behind
the sky. Then followed smacking thunder, then rain
that roared like wild applause of crowds a million
strong; and Tol, unseeing in the deluge,
felt the pador's hand hold his and tug him,
wading, through a trail of leaves that swelled with
water faster than it filtered to the
forest floor below. Then, where three trails met,
Tol dimly heard and saw, a rapid whirlpool
coiled sharply down; and with no chance to flee
the surging flood, they spun into its grasp.

Tol felt, mid-plummet, the pador's paw-like
hand grab his and pull him to a woven
pallet of dead vines, which, levered by some
unseen counterweight and burdened by the
pador, Human and the spiralled torrent,
drifted down, cracking, to the rain-soaked ground
below. Descended thus, they made their way
among the trees until, quite soon, they stood
before a mighty river's swirling waves.
Some miles downstream aboard the pador's
deftly handled boat, the sky appeared above
an Attatrulan town, where they engaged
the transport of a blue-green carriage bird,
this mode of movement being common all

throughout that world. Some hours deeply nestled
in its feathered neck, lightly burnt by sun
and wind, these two at last arrived,
beyond the forest's edge, at Crater Krel.

Clutching one strong feather to keep aboard
the bird, the pador leaned her body's length
to wave a hand within the creature's view.
Its black and glossy twelve-foot eye's response,
unblinking, was to search a place to land.
Six miles across, the Crater Krel sank deeply
from the bending forest trees that circled,
like eyelashes, all around the dead
and empty socket of its lifeless,
silent waste. The crater had been formed,
some few millennia ago, upon
the impact of a meteor of salt,
whose sharp exploded bits prevented life
from growing, even from the fecund soil
of Attatrul: here, the bird set down its feet.

"Can it be Tol, and Videvis, have come
to find me hiding in this salty hole?"
A voice erupted sharply from within
a rock-strewn place. "Come here and speak so that
yourselves are known to my small sightless self."

Tol turned and saw Parinmawada's smile
glowing from the top of its small form,
comical, squat, and tilted motionless,
as if too long no pador had been there

to keep the helpless Kowd from shifting in
the windswept, barren soil. Surprised, Tol spoke:
"By all the planets where our Species live,
no joy could equal seeing you today.
Great gladness swells my inmost self like
water poured across a sundried sponge: hail your
wisdom, Parinmawada, friend of mine!"
"Calm yourself. Some sober news awaits you,"
said the Kowd, as its voice became quite grave.
"Ask no questions. At this time, you must hear
and learn my words in this so desolate
a place, this aberration in a universe
untouched by natural calamity.
To you, my words will not seem true,
especially when I ask you to accept
that words may be untrue—but mine are not.
Go, Videvis, good pador, take your rest."
To these words of the limbless Kowd, Tol said:
"It is quite rare that any Kowd will speak,
and rarer still that anyone should want
to bring a dislocated hermit, as
myself, to where, it seems, you seek to bury
secrets in the harshness of this salt.
But I must know, and tell me, how it is
you and Videvis could know I would arrive
on this lush world of greenness when I did;
and what's more, what brings you to Attatrul—
you, whose blissful meditations lasted

years amid the peace of gurgling silver streams?
Lastly, tell me, Kowd, whether meeting you
fits into strange events which have beset
myself, Asara and our silver world,
and whether you have knowledge of what only
she and I can know—and dare not say—
the happening that made me seek the starbeam's sleep."

"Hear me!" Parinmawada sharply spoke.
"Do not make me repeat that you must ask
no questions. Accept that what you hear is
for your ears and that you need know nothing
but what I shall say. Promise, now, to hear."

Gravely puzzled, the Human slowly said,
"As all life is right and good, I shall hear;
and I shall learn, if you will teach me, how
this 'falsehood' truly is what is not true."

"All space, the universe," began the Kowd,
"has origins so dim, and past remote,
the Higher Species have, for unnumbered
millennia, directed all their tasks,
and thoughts, to building for the future and
the present, and to reconstructing only,
for the curious amusement that it brings,
such past events as memory reveals.
All our recollections are near dead.
Yet Tersai, Kowd and Human tales, each with
nuances, angles, treatments, points of view
peculiar to each teller of each tale,

together give us history. This you know;
and were it gathered to one place, and with
a thousand books inscribed upon each particle
of denser matter than is known,
the weight would shift, from orbit, any world.

"Perhaps it is the sheerest volume of
the content of our past that wearies us,
before we even start, in that great task
of learning where and what we all have been
and done. Where to begin, with memories, books
and records faded well past all repair?
Yet from the heaving shoals of detail from
the past, great waves break wide across the
level passive shores of our ability
to recall, to explain, and to live on.
Thus, infinite intersections of time—
these droplets—crash foaming as an event.
Know this, that seven such events give us
the base, and superstructure, of our past.

"First came the Era of the Aliadni,
followed by the First Great Abolition
when we survived the sure demise of death;
third, there came the Age of Endless Wars;
fourth, the Second Abolition, and then
the Age of Art. Sixth was the Flowering
of the Centratrees; and finally, therc
came the fruit those flowers brought among us,
the present, and the greatest, Age of Love.

From causes unexplained, the story of
the Aliadni times, when death still lived,
has vanished from the records and the minds
of those, like you and me, who, born to flesh,
lived on to know death die—and thus became
the ones we call the Aliadni,
the procreators, by forgotten Craft,
of all the rest of all three Higher Species.

"But I, yourself and others have applied
much time to mending broken threads of time;
and plainly as my words can tell you now,
this is what happened then, so long ago:

"Three sets of Beings, governments and lives,
who—named then as now, Tersai, Human, Kowd—
inhabited three small parts of what is
now known space. At that time, all three Species
had the will and clever, fast machines
to fight among themselves, and with each other,
like animals competing for their food,
except, it seems, they needed no excuse
to fight—and fought for reasons hung from rings
of smoke. Emotions, then, were different, too;
and my restitching shreds of those lost days
suggests that what we now would know as deep
suspense was something then called 'fear'; and fear
was having thoughts of harm which could not be
undone. A simple thought of being
disinclined took then a harsh and ugly form

in something they called 'hatred.' Emulation,
when impossible, became 'jealousy';
and our spreading spectrum of concern
broke then in sordid colors of 'anguish,'
'anger' and 'worry.' While they did have love,
our forebears had less time for its pursuit.
They, of necessity, were occupied
with things called 'evils,' now to us unknown;
and evils filled their days. Most demanding
of their time were sickness, crime and money:
impairments of their bodies, of their motives,
and of their will to trust each other.

"Much of this, Tol, will be for you obscure
and without meaning. Nonetheless, my dark
exhumation of what life was like, when
Higher Species yielded to the terrors
of the animals, requires that you
also know of what the ancients knew as
'murder.' Consider, first, what it was
to die: to depart, and be not present,
yet go nowhere, dream no sleep, and arrive
no place, and disappear digested into
nothingness, not to be part of time,
no further breath, no merest thought, no life.

"Next, reflect upon the doing of an act
intended to deprive a fellow Being
of its life—to plan, then do, what will end
the breathing of another like oneself,

who then will die and nevermore reflect
on living or on dying. This occurred.
Yet until recent efforts by myself,
and others, this incomprehensible
dark secret of the Higher Species' past
was hidden and unknown. With this knowledge,
it now seems we must adopt the ancient
term called 'horror' to describe our
own but distant past, the faded past that
near infinite betterments of what
we are, and do, have pressed into the cramped
and inaccessible spaces of
irrelevancy. Now, with this in mind,
let me retell for you, with more detail,
the story of the Ages of our past.

"The Era of the Aliadni starts
so long ago we cannot even guess.
There is no world, no place, no artifact,
that has survived from those most distant years.
By gathering all knowledge of our point
in time, I have, by Craft and meditation,
tried extrapolation to the past;
and this has brought most startling results.
The Higher Species, in those shrouded times,
lived no more than several hundred years apiece.
To maintain their species, the Humans and
the Tersai obtained replacement Beings,
by union of their sexes, in the act

which both those Species still enjoy. The Kowd
did not pursue this thing called birth—instead,
when passing years had overcome the lives
of bodies subject to the rot which yet
dissolves the lower species and the plants,
each dead Kowd was buried in a place where
soon appeared a little bush, whose leaves, when
brewed in tea, turned certain lower species
who consumed it, through some unknown process,
into new, limbless, sexless, sightless Kowd.

"We have some knowledge where our forebears
lived. The Kowd had always lived upon the giant,
desert planets spinning wide around
a white-hot star called Toor. The Tersai lived
not many Centrayears of lightspeed thence.
The Humans came from still uncertain planets,
somewhere within Stellar Sector Two,
and sang sad songs about a world called Earth.
All else about beginnings is obscure.

"We do know that these Species met, in travels
through deep space, recoiling with such fear,
as I've explained this term, that each resolved
to seek the murder of the others in what
then was known as 'war.' For many years,
vast starship navies circled and positioned
for one final lightening strike, one last drive
to terminate their foe and live to see
them die. We do not know—may never know—

what intervened to stop this race to death,
although it seems to have arisen from
a mystic force, derived from merging thought,
that was touched off when these three Species met.
Whatever was the reason, or the cause,
of this the First Great Abolition, its
effect was sudden, strong and universal:
the end of pain, of birth, of aging,
of hunger, sexuality and death—
and, with these, was also then abolished
the memory and knowledge of what life
was like before this so great change. So, Tol,
thus darkened all the Aliadni minds.

"This great abolition also touched the
padors, the servant beasts who always served
us limbless Kowd as mobile second selves;
and they, like us, lived on and do not die.

"The end of death took place in several forms:
the Tersai bodies, at that time, became
not only strong, but indestructible.
No known force can tear, or break, or hurt
or make the slightest mark on any Tersai form.
However, all the Humans, Kowd and padors
still remained exposed to hurt, except
that, powered by the force of gravity,
a process of revival, or of healing,
as circumstance required, began restoring

all the bodies of those species every
time when harm or damage would occur.
"Along with this protection from all death,
there also came deliverance from all pain.
A Tersai plunged in flame felt only heat.
The Humans and the padors still retained
some portion of a strong, reactive pull
that draws back sharply from all harm to flesh.
We Kowd, in keeping with our kind, lost almost
all sensation, except that in our minds.
For all four species, the rage of hunger
and starvation quickly eased, receding
to reminding pangs that tell us when to eat
and which, if left unheeded for too long,
inflict no more than slight discomfort, while
our bodies feed on thought itself for food.
While hunger softened, birth and aging ceased:
the entrances and exits to our four
dimensions then became forever blocked;
and we all came to be an average age.
The young grew up. The old grew young again.
"These new events forestalled the threat of war;
and uncontrolled rejoicing must have filled
the hearts of all; and every Higher Being
must have felt good will, celebrating, at last,
deliverance from the tyrant reign of death,
at least until all minds closed off, in all
of us, the memory of what we were.

For some time, all was peace; and wherever
in deep space the Higher Species met,
we traded with each other all our customs,
thoughts and dreams, our manners, habits, ways,
and, maybe most importantly, our
total store of science. As knowledge combined,
our scientific strivings soon produced
what, separately, they never had and never
could achieve: the lightspeed travel of
the starbeam's sleep; and this and other marvels
of collected science we called Craft.

"Next, we thought the Higher Species could
combine their efforts and explore all space in peace.
In all directions, we suffused the
empty reaches, making atmospheres on
planets which had none, drifting patiently
asleep, along the starbeam's path, until
the twinkle of the distant stars became
our noonday heat—but, when we discovered
worlds of beauty vaster and more numerous
than we could populate, we overcame
the end of birth; and we created,
by Craft, more new Tersai and more Humans
than any desert planet's flecks of dust.
These new Beings filled the depths of space with life."

"But why, Parinmawada," Tol spoke up,
"did you Kowd refuse to reproduce?

Even now, all Kowd are Aliadni,
since each lived when doors to death were shut."

"Your questions slow my story. Hold your
tongue," the tiny Kowd replied, and then pressed on
to end its tale: "You, Tol, should be aware,
more than any Being in all space, how
often one's desires crumble into sand.
It happened still more often in those days.
The plan to spread the Higher Species outward,
through the stars, became within the fewest
thousand years a plan by each—the Tersai,
Human, Kowd—to take the best position
to begin, and win, a war to conquer space.
Release from death had brought with it
the prospect, for each Higher Being,
of eternity at work, at labor
to plant seeds, grow food, collect it in and
share it all around; to build our homes,
our cities, bridges, roads; to make,
as well, our clothes and shoes. The exit from
this bondage lay, most clearly it then seemed,
within enslaving others to all tasks,
taking from them freedom for oneself,
to be thus lord of everything but boredom.

"Once again, the tactics drawn, positions
taken, ambitions breathed and vengeance sought,
all Beings of the Higher Species poised
to fight. This time was mighty war declared,

and there was mighty war. Strategies of
all three sides collided with fantastic
complexity, as armies, numerous
as stars, deflected through deep space from
starbeam post to starbeam post. Droves of captives,
in this deathless war, sat huddled on
a thousand prison planets—all in cold and
silent fear of eternal slavery.

"The war progressed to where there soon would
happen either final climax, or stalemate.
The Kowd, despite how few we were, had cornered
Human forces so that no escape
could be, except for one good chance to press
the Tersai to surrender. This last chance
improved, tenfold, when it appeared the Tersai
had converted key defenses to
attack the Kowd positions with a threat
of sure defeat. By some coincidence,
tacticians for each side concluded that
the last assault should start by massing forces
in the shadows of Kolku, a near dead
giant star whose central place, and heavy belt
of asteroids for starbeam posts, made it
the highest ground. Long years passed as armies
crept at lightspeed, fast asleep, to this place
of final war. Yet none would venture close,
or set a foot on any asteroid;
for mighty storms of particle winds

were raging round the death throes of Kolku;
and some asteroids were then exploding
without warning. The Kowd and Humans feared
to be destroyed beyond the reach of any
planet's life-renewing gravity.
The Tersai feared they would be blown adrift
and lost forever, shot through empty space.

"As more and more, the mighty forces poured
upon the planets of the stars around
Kolku, and when the time for battle had
arrived, and just when in each camp impatience
was converting all the fearful to
be brave, a stronger force than any army
intervened to stop that day of war.

"Unknown to almost any at that time,
some small groups of each, the Species three,
had banded with each other in the task
of using Craft to cure the ills of war—
and to this end, they for the first time built
the languages and incantations, which,
when harmonized with Craft, brought new matter
into being; and so there came to be,
from creative thought alone, substance.
This new thought, together with the armies,
converged in waves upon the dimming region
of Kolku. There, the poised and savage
forces witnessed the formation, out of

purest nothing, of the planet we call
Centra, the largest planet in known space.
"The Craft and incantations of that day
restored, as well, Kolku to brightest fire,
which warmed the Centran mountains and its plains.
Right at the center of one vast plateau,
the excess of this new creative force
erupted as a voice from solid rock,
the voice of the Oracle, the Great and
Universal Source, the voice that rules all space.
"There was then a sudden peace; and, to those
assembled awestruck on that wide plateau,
the voice declared in solemn tones that this
was peace that would not end, that war would be
no more, that nevermore would any Higher
Species think or do an evil thing,
nor would the world of nature do us harm.
This then was the Second Abolition.
"Except for one loud rock, from deep in space,
that made this place of salt where we now sit,
the peace that followed is unbroken to
this day. For countless millennia
of Centrayears, as measured by the slow
and lazy orbit of that world around
Kolku, the Higher Species turned a new
collective hand to searching out the limits
of their creative mind. Guided by
the terse pronouncements which, from time to time,

were uttered by the Source, and managed by
the government that formed to do its will,
the Humans and the Tersai and the Kowd
designed, and then created, many worlds,
and after time, by Craft, created also stars,
weaving, through the galaxies, new solar
systems like a cloth of fine spun gold.

"We knew this time as the Great Age of Art;
for by design artistic was the shape
of space remade; and, Tol, as you well know,
the last events of this Great Age were your
world of silver streams, and Attatrul, and
their double suns whose fire gives them life.

"The details of what happened, after this
Great Age of Art, are so well known and often
celebrated, in our feasting and our dance,
that little need be said. As sung in songs
and told in fables, there came a day when
all the trees around the Source at Centra
put forth blooms the like of which no one had
ever seen; and though the stories differ
who it was, and how it came about,
someone soon discovered that the eating
of these leaves awakened, in the Humans
and the Tersai both, the long dead feelings
in their loins which had lain dormant for so long.

"The resurrection of the sport of sex
enveloped all known space in pilgrimage

to Centra. Even many Kowd set out
to span deep space and share the taste of love,
although, of course, our bodies cannot play
your sweating game of grunts and thrusts and moans.
The Age of Love had dawned and brought its warmth
of dreamy, languid hours, which have yet to end.
"Of all this story I have told you, Tol,
some is history, some informed conjecture,
and some is truth once missing but now found.
Yet other parts come sifting through a screen
of hazy vision that enmeshed my years
of sightless thought; and what has lately reached
me makes me understand this ancient thing
called fear. Far off, in Stellar Sector Five,
my vision spoke, the long-forgotten myth
of death, affecting Higher Species, has
invaded present time, has ended many
lives, and has, by witness of the vacant
bodies in that place, turned myth to fact.
I cried, 'Untrue, this is impossible,'
but this same vision then told me that Tol
would soon arrive—and that there would be rain.
I sent my pador. She returned with you.
Tell me, Tol, can there truly be untruth?"
"My dear closest friend, Parinmawada,"
said Tol, as if he were exhaling for
the first time since the Kowd began to speak,
"my mind is flooded with your so strange words.

I am here because I built, at last, my
crystal table, through which the Source told me
to come. The wife of our planetlord
is mute, and secrecy is all the reason
given for the travel, Centrabound,
of Bal. Your deathly vision reaches past
concern. Surely these events can only
be resolved upon Oracular direction.
There should soon be a pronouncement."

Agreed on this, Tol and the Kowd reflected
for some silent moments. Tol then beckoned to
the pador, who was marking her initial,
as a V shaped trench, upon the sand.

The double suns were setting as they left,
and pools of darkness swelled among the hills.
The wind, in gusts, churned up the sand and dust
which sunlight had reclaimed from clogging rain.
Within the V, by paws of pador made,
and within hearing of where Tol had stood,
the streaming sand wore down to show a face
in outlines barely seen in that last light.
The face belonged to Ito, the Human
Centran Envoy of the Source, who heard all.

The Chasm

Chapter 4

The Chasm

Swarms of noisy thoughts receded at the
place where Tol lay down to sleep. His friend,
the Kowd, had understood when Tol departed
through the woods, alone, to find a quiet,
soft and mossy place. Sleep came soon and pressed
him into muffled depths and dark retreat.

Not long before the first bird sang the dawn,
invading dreams besieged his peaceful rest.
Image followed restless image until
he was awake—and then was kept awake
by efforts to decide what thoughts to think.
His breath came short as through his heavy-
lidded eyes he watched the rising double
orange fires flashing westward through the leaves;
and while all the forest quickened into

life, Tol wished that he had only dreamed
a thing called fear about a thing called death.
He found a path that took him through the hills
that rolled in wooden waves away from
Crater Krel. He did not feel or hear the fronds
of saplings wash against his pacing legs,
for all his focused thought was of Asara.
Before he left his world of silver streams,
the two of them had sworn a noble love,
a love to be, between them, always strong
and true. To heed the Source and its clear words,
Tol came directly to the world where now
he walked. Asara travelled straight to Olsta's
small thatched home. Yet, before they parted,
Asara said, embracing Tol, that she
would join him soon, on Planet Attatrul,
and share in all uncertainties to come.
She first must find what robbed her friend of speech.
A morning's walk behind him, Tol approached
a thickening of trees; and there in total
shadows, at a wall of branches and dead leaves,
the trail completely stopped and went no more.
At several hundred feet above Tol's head,
a glint of greenish blue revealed a patch
of Attatrulan sky. From this small gap,
a length of vine reached downward in a loop.
At Tol's touch, it moved, one side up, the other

down; and borne upon a knotted foothold,
he rose up to the treetop world above.

The nameless trail resumed and reached its
winding length to intersections of a dozen paths.
Once joined, they widened to broad, level
walkways made of interlocking planks of
polished amber wood. As he walked, the horizon
shouldered soon the steeply gabled
clusters which were structures of a town,
the Attatrulan village called Bandoo.

The merriment of music and good cheer
encircled Tol when, from his thoughts, he stepped
into the gated streets and felt their festive
pulse. In Bandoo, that day, there was joy.
A hundred jugglers spun around the square.
Ten Tersai men and women, dressed in red,
bore on their shoulders, without any strain,
an acre's size of wooden stage; and on
this stage, pairs and groups of merry padors
frolicked, danced and played to music blown from
horns and plucked from strings and measured from the
surface of a drum. Banners, flags and ensigns
billowed rippling colors in the breeze;
and over parkland walkways, all around the
wooden stage, a loose parade of pipers,
acrobats and clowns made improvised
processions through the crowds. Amid the noise
and color moved the ghost-like form of Tol.

Wheeled on silver wheels, and pushed by twenty
Tersai women barely dressed in tiny scarves,
a massive seashell, thirty feet across,
bore in its rosy mouth the Planet's lord—
Ilka, Lady Lord and sovereign of that world.
The shell had been a gift to her, given
by one of many suitors who, throughout
the centuries, had sought her hand to wed.
She kept the shell and used it as a throne.
Its donor she sent disappointed home—
perhaps because she felt no love for him,
or, as likely, since she had already
taken many mates—as long had been the
custom on that world—and had more husbands
than the leisure time to know them well.

A Tersai man asked Tol where he was from;
and learning that Tol had, just now, arrived,
the Tersai whispered news the village had
a visitor, who should be properly
received. The giant shell came up to where
they stood and halted. The music stopped mid-note,
and dancers froze, when Ilka raised her voice:

"Our joy today is doubled; for not only
do our wooden streets resound with festive
noise to mark the Attatrulan northern spring,
we now also have a visitor to
share our happy day. Tol, I welcome you
and bid you be as one of us today."

"O Planetlord of great renown," said Tol,
"I take this honor, and I share your joy.
Accept my thanks, together with my praise
of your great beauty and that of this world."
"What brings you to the Attatrulan woods?"
inquired Ilka with the spreading smile
which long had branded many hearts with love.
"I bear the burden of such vast concerns
that I must seek permission not to pierce
your frothy gladness with my stony cares."
Tol wondered why he looked upon the ground.
"As Centra rules all space," replied Ilka,
with her smile in retreat, "what do you say?
How can there be concern or care to mar
a day of joy, for care is part of all
responsibility, which is a joy to fill.
Speak now, Tol, and explain your mind."
Truth, once demanded, could only then be
speech. Tol looked at her and said, "I fell in love.
The dearest friend of my dear spouse, for no
reason that I know, lost her speech and may
not use her tongue. All such matters unexplained
require words from Centra; and impatience
overcame my will to live the law of Bal,
our planet's lord. I marshalled Craft to learn
directly what the Source would say. I was
directed to come here, and so I came."

Tol then had to pause until an urgent
murmur had died down. All Beings were amazed
their visitor had heard the Source itself.
When silence gathered, Tol continued on.

"My friend, a worthy Kowd, told me it learned
the Higher Species, at one time long past
before our memory began, were subject
to the stone-cold termination of
a lower species' life. It also said
that such strange complexity may now have
recommenced, afar, in Stellar Sector Five.
I want to think this through and what this terse
direction from the Source may mean. For this,
I feel I must retire from you all."

Several seconds passed before new silence broke
with Ilka's voice: "I cannot comprehend
the sequence of your words. Neither can I
fathom how you have supreme command of law
which was unlawfully obtained. Stranger
still unfold your words that any Higher
Being could know death. There has been error here,
or misinterpretation, or some fault
arising from a pador's inattention.
Yet, let it not be said that we upon
this wooden world refused to heed the Great
and Universal Source—and everything
oracular direction may imply.
If you believe you must seek solitude,

then ride upon my carriage bird, and go
and seek the quiet of my now deserted
summer house, which, though large, has been long since
too small to house me and my many mates.
While I would as soon accept that I could now
surpass the speed of light as contemplate
my death, I must assist you and the Source."

With that, a somber Tersai woman of
uncommon strength, even for that Species,
stepped from the crowd. She pursed her lips and
whistled one long blast, as piercing as a shriek;
and while this summons stirred the royal feathered
mount to leave its hundred-meter nest,
and crush the wind, and pound the air in flight,
then soar above the town, this Tersai fixed
her hands on Tol. With one blurred graceful thrust,
she propelled the Human up to meet
the diving bird, whose broad back arrested him
just as his high ascent became his fall.

The bird and Tol shot off in wild haste.
Behind the streaks of speeding clouds below,
between his wind-drawn tears, Tol squinting saw
the surface of the planet angle sharply
upward to the skies and strangely end.
From books about mistakes and errors in
the use of Craft, he knew they neared the
wondrous Chasm of Logall, which cut its S-shaped
trench, abruptly, through the bulging land mass

that had formed when the planet's largest
moon had lost its orbit, plunged half its screaming
shape beneath the sea, some distance from
the shore, and cracked in two. This chasm lay
so deep and far across, its bottom and
its other side could not be seen. Instead,
the unassisted eye searched helplessly
among the air-distorted hues and shapes,
stitched into seamless carpetings and
tapestries of mist. Tol felt the air grow cold
and thin, and he concluded that the bird
had flown him near the savage summit of
that mountained moon. When both huge claws had
lodged into the ground and made secure the
feathered hulk, Tol saw he was at Ilka's house.
It overlooked a melting ice field at
the chasm's edge, from which a steady spray
of water fell into the dim abyss
towards the unseen ocean arm below.

The bird departed, and he was alone.
Some padors, sent at Ilka's bidding, came
to tend to him, but he sent them all away.
Days came and went like clouds of vapor,
forming once, then seeming to have never been.

One soft evening, at dusk, the double orange
glow had all but vanished, and the stars
began to spark. Strange echoes of the sea,
or of the wind, glanced off the chasm walls.

Tol stood upon a small high deck and watched
the largest star, the silver one, his home.
He looked until he thought he saw, upon
that star, Asara's face; and he smiled
and thought that time had come to go to bed.
He turned to go, but still the image of
his Tersai lover stayed before his eyes.
The face's head appeared and then the torso
and the limbs he knew so well. With discomfort
in this waking dream, he spoke her name out loud:
"Asara! How does your person come before
me now? Have you, somehow, by starbeam come?"
"It's me. I'm here," the image spoke to him.
She grew opaque; and as she did, a veil
of purple, borne upon the wind, slid round
her form, which now appeared to walk along
the deck. "I am the beauty which you love;
and how I come to you, you need not know—
no more than you need know why you were sent
to dwell within this Attatrulan place.
Come here and kiss me." She stepped towards him.
She pressed her lips and self against him in
a manner wanting more. Tol felt his body
yielding to this familiar soft embrace,
familiar smell and touch and so fine shape,
except he did not sense from her the hidden
unused reservoirs of might that was
her Tersai strength. He pushed her back from him.

Asara's buoyant features slowly fell
into what Parinmawada's research
knew as sadness. She chewed her lip and breathed
a sigh. Motionless, silent, Tol watched her.

"Tol, look out at the sky," she said, "and see
the planet which, for both of us, is home.
Look at it as you looked at me, just now,
when first you saw my face." Tol obeyed her
and turned toward the speckled nighttime sky.
"Now, close your eyes, and tell me what you see."

"I still can see our silver planet's glow,"
said Tol, his eyes now firmly shut, "but it
is not the same. It grows larger, nearer,
more intense in brightness until, until...."

These were his only words for quite some time.
He sat down and rocked and moaned and shook
his head, and he grasped at phantoms in the air.
The wind died down. More stars came out, and there
was total silence, save for the eerie
thunder of the melted waters tumbling
off the cliff and into rain. Then, he spoke.

"My sweet Asara, as you seem to be,
as Centra rules all space, what corrosion
do you cast upon the tissues of my mind?
Just now, behind my eyelids, there occurred
one flashing blast that filled the sky and was
the final sure destruction of our world.
I cannot even think the thing I saw:

a shining planet, then combusting light
to each horizon's end, and then nothing.
Yet, looking now, I see our world endures."

"Consider what you've seen," Asara said.
"You are a Human, and your body knows
no harm, for any damage to it swiftly
heals. Yet this repair occurs by force
exerted from all planets' innate mass.
As gravity gives weight, this force gives health
and restoration to the Humans and
the Kowd. The body of a Tersai knows
no hurt. Think of a planet's destruction.
Think of Kowd and Humans exploded
into bits, permanently, and Tersai cast
forever drifting, alive, alone and lost."

"You are not, and cannot be, Asara,"
Tol said, circling beyond her reach. "Tell me
how you appear to be what you are not."

Asara whispered in response, "Come here
and face your truest love of many vows.
Accept what is, as Centra rules all space."
She gestured to him in Asara's way
of offering herself. "Come here and take
my body's pleasure while it may be had."

Tol, for a moment, yearned to grasp her
ready form. He hesitated, then spoke:
"Of all the things we know, the surest is
that how love happens to us is not known.

Neither can we figure how this force, which
follows us through space from those bright Centratrees,
can sometimes quickly end; but know this:
my love for you is over. Please, now, go."

Asara's face contorted and then changed
completely. Just where his lover stood, there
now appeared the Human Centran Envoy,
Ito, who watched with sharp and narrow looks
Tol's sudden strong discomfort and surprise.

"Be not now confused," she said, "and hear my
story. My name is Ito, and I have
great power. I am sent here by the Source,
and you were sent to meet me here and do
my will. You see that I can change how things
appear. From this, infer what has been granted
to me by the Source. You are to help me
use this gift. I, not Centra, will rule all space."

"I have been told," said Tol, "that in the past
the Higher Species spoke in words that were
not true. You speak truth and falsehood both.
True it is, the Source has sent me here;
but that it was to serve a strange mirage
such as yourself, whose very substance is
in doubt, I cannot accept. Can you say
why I should hear more of what you say?"

"You know of falsehood. Do you also know
of death?" asked Ito in reply. "If you
fail now to do my will and come with me,

your breathing and your thinking will soon cease.
I know more about you even than yourself,
and you must trust that I and only I
can keep you from the permanence of death.
I have approached you as I did because
you matter more than means to reach an end.
I have followed you, and I have watched you,
and without wanting to, I have fallen
hard in love with you. Hear this. This is truth.
Will you now come and rule all space with me?"

"Some machines," said Tol, "are propelled by
gears, which, when worn by friction, bring about
strange random movements that make no sense at all.
If you are a Higher Being, then you
could have no such defect. I conclude you
are a thing mechanical, broken,
or else a freakish play of light and sound
which has escaped this chasm's deep unknown."
Tol wondered, though, how Ito knew that he
was sent to Attatrul and also why
he felt, somehow, attracted by her words.

"I will now go," said Ito, with her hands
upon her hips, "but please remember this:
all truth is only what is proven true.
You have refused me. Therefore, your Planet
of the Silver Streams shall be destroyed.
Events will prove my words; and if you say
to anyone what I have said to you,

or even mention that we met, then you
shall cause the final end of other worlds."

With that, she vanished. The purple veil was
caught by gusting winds and carried to the
chasm's depth. Moments later, there arrived
at Ilka's house the pador Videvis,
who, seeing Tol's discomfort and concern,
invited him to walk down through the woods
to watch a quiet pond reflect the stars.
They went. Close by the pond, Tol sat, observing
the reflected silver dot that was
his world. The pador lost her balance with
alarm, but Tol remained unflinching as
they watched the silver planet come apart
and bathe the sky in sparks—this time for real.

The Meteor

Chapter 5

The Meteor

The nighttime sky of Attatrul was far
too small to frame the blinding picture of
its neighbour planet's end. First, laser beacons
from the forces of ignition laced
the sky in sparkling threads. Then, as Tol's world
became a pulsing ball of fire, the night
became as day, and then too bright for day,
until all colors paled to white and shadows
fled and nothing could be seen at all.
Behind the lingered flash, in silence of
deep space, the world of silver blew apart.

Most Higher Beings on the darkened side
of Attatrul were wakened by the light
and went outside to look. Their telescopes
and calculations told them that, just half

an afternoon of lightspeed from their world,
a planet full of beauty met its end.
Ilka and her Counsellors of Craft convened
by telescreen. Nothing could be done,
they soon resolved, to bring back any Tersai
flung into the emptiness of space
with greater speed than any rescue ship
could go. The Kowd and Human bodies,
blasted into ruin, were most surely
beyond help. What else to do or think would have
to wait the next pronouncement from the Source.

In amazement, Tol wondered at the sick
and troubled wave that broke throughout his
agitated self. He reasoned that his lover
and his planet, which were his total future
and his past, were now to be no more.
Yet none of his emotions was conditioned
to confront a loss without repair.
His body shook and ached as this lone Human
tried to feel what once was called despair.

The sky soon cleared, and all the stars returned.
The sudden blindness of ten thousand eyes
on Attatrul, including Tol's, soon healed.
With sight restored, he looked out at the patch
of violet sky where once had shone his world,
then looked across the waters of the pond.
He pulled the pador to her feet and spoke.

"My Videvis, the sight we saw tonight
gives proof to words that gave me fear of proof.
This Ito knows why I am on this world.
She also knew, before the fact, that my
Asara, and everyone I knew and
loved, would cease. She asked me to go with her.
Have I refused to follow what the Source
has said? Have I now caused this ruin in
the sky? Asara said that I should seek
the Source; and this I did, learning then that
some petition, I know not what, would be
denied. Until all this has been explained
and there has been direction from the Source,
I will not know what life has done to me."

His voice trailed off, and raspy-throated insects
marked the surface of the water into
patterns with no plan. The pador lay
her head upon her paws and looked up at
the stars. From far within the tangled woods,
a long, slow, steady howling shared some nameless
lower species' deep and faceless gloom.

Not long before the heat of dawn set fire
to its edge, the sky began to sparkle.
Points of light, one here, one there, and some
in groups like showers of salt, began to bring
the sky to life once more. The pador stirred,
and Tol looked up to see this new alarm.
They watched the fiery pinholes flash and die,

then burn and fade more slowly from their sight;
and then, at length, one flaming mass emerged,
far brighter than the rest. It streaked across
the sky. Then all his wonderment gave way
to knowledge that he watched stray remnants of
his planet burn to cinders, as they pierced
the atmospheric layers overhead.

Then, as she had before, the pador
seized his hand and pulled him with a purpose
down along a path. Again, Tol followed her.
The brighter falling star continued burning
as they ran full speed toward an unseen goal.
The path turned upwards, steeply; and they
soon emerged where melting waters from
the towered peaks rolled outward to the chasm's
darkness and beyond. A tail of burning
gases spiralled out behind the fast
approaching mass, and Tol and Videvis
could see that its great impact would be soon.

The thing slammed hard into the sloping side
of one large mountain at the chasm's edge.
The impact shuddered downwards through a wide
and shining vein of soft metallic ore
where it had struck. The crater was not large.
The blasted rock and dust mixed through the swirling
morning haze and marked, in air, the place
of this event. The pador then led on,
up to the crater's lip, where oxidizing

pools of molten metal glistened, in
concentric furrows, all around the deep
and smoking blackness where the meteor
struck down. Tol wondered what the pador sought.

Then Tol grew pale to hear faint sounds of
speaking echo up from deep within the hole.
"Whose is that voice? Who calls us from below?"
he asked, and, turning, saw the pador scamper
off through leafless bushes and dead trees.

"Hello! Anyone there? Hello!" the voice
was shouting in a thick and raspy tone.
It sounded vaguely female to Tol's ears.

"Speak up!" Tol cried, "can you get out?
You must need help. I cannot cross to where
your voice comes from, for I am Human, and my legs
would burn and break among the flames surrounding
where you are." He stood upon his toes
and strained to see down in the hole.

A hand appeared, reaching out and clawing
through the burning ground to find a solid hold.
The hand was charred and streaked with bluish ash,
and likewise was the balance of the female
form that crawled out of the dirt. A Tersai,
Tol concluded with amazement, had fallen
from the sky—but with so slight an impact
and such remoteness of the chance, it seemed
to him this could not be a Higher Being
blasted from his silver world to here.

The Tersai female stood and tried to wipe
the ashes from her eyes. Her hair and clothes
had burnt entirely away, although
some pieces, here and there, seemed to have
melted and then fused onto her scorched
and mottled skin. Tol was startled then to hear
this Being speak in his Asara's voice.

"Tol, as Centra rules all space, your face
is joy to me like mighty rocks that never
yield to any power of the changing sea.
I would embrace you, but my skin is yet
so hot that you would flash to cinders in
my arms. Speak now, and let me hear your voice."

Tol paused and stared. "Are you," he said,
"that one who speaks in voices set in bodies not
her own and with one word destroys a world?"

"I am your love, and very little is
there, my Tol, that you do not know of me.
What would persuade you I am she you know?"

Tol asked where she had been, and she
replied, "Since we last spoke among the shattered
crystals of your Craft, I went to my friend, Olsta.
First, she would not let me in her room;
but through the door, I spoke to her, recalling
all our pleasant times of trust and care
and talk. She let me in. She did not speak,
and so I gave her paper and a pen
to write her thoughts. This she refused, and then

I knew she self-imposed her verbal exile.
I asked her then to come with me, to look
for you upon this world of Attatrul.
She nodded yes; but as we squinting stood,
upon the diamond floor at Caves of
Starbeams' Rest, and were, by half, dissociated
from our material state, one great roar
of noise and wind rushed through. The last we saw
of our bright silver home was fire and smoke
and melting granite walls. My next waking
thought was on the mounted platform of
a satellite in Attatrulan orbit.
Whatever happened, as we left, had caused
our beam to angle from its mark and come
to rest upon that piece of metal in
the sky, which never was designed to take
a starbeam from its path. I woke to see
that Olsta's body was, by this event,
quite badly broken. She was freezing solid
in the temperature of space. Although,
of course, I was myself intact, I could
not, without air, continue movement for
much time; and so within my gulp of air
transported from our world, I found and fired
ancient jets that pushed us and the spinning
metal bird towards this world of wood.

"I pressed the limits of my Tersai strength
to clutch dear Olsta, shielding her

frail Human form from burning all to ash
before we reached the gravitation which
restores all Human flesh. This is the last
that I recall before this planet's air
could penetrate the smoke in that small hole
from where I have just now emerged, waking
me to the great surprise of seeing you.
Who is it speaks in bodies not her own?"

Tol said nothing but gestured to the stream
that ran nearby. Asara went; and when
her body cooled and ceased to churn the water
into steam, she scraped her form with porous
rocks that lay in shallow pools. Thus cleansed,
she took from Tol his outer clothes and smiling
thought how she must look without her hair.

"Do you," asked Tol, "think any part of Olsta's
fragile body has survived this fall?"

"I cannot tell," Asara said, "but this
small pile of caked-on soot and layered ash,
which came off me, should yet contain some bits
of what she was. I feel quite certain that
these cinders hold her essence in a stasis
that endures. Apply your Craft and see."

The two of them set out for Ilka's house
and brought the scorched remains, all wrapped
in cloth. Asara found some clothes, and Tol
collected all the usual ingredients
to reconstruct a Human from the

scantiest of remains. He then combined
the chemistry of these with well-worn
incantations, and the movements of a dance,
until he was relieved to see the product
of his Craft—for those dead embers grew
and breathed to be his planetlord's dear spouse,
who, out of almost nothing, was made whole.
"Olsta, now, please talk," implored Asara
to her newly remade friend. "You have
returned from the unknown, the unthinkable
prospect of destruction beyond the power
of gravity to bring back Human flesh.
Now speak, and tell your friends that you are glad."
Olsta exhaled slowly and bowed her head.
The bright fires, twins of the noonday sky
above them where they sat on Ilka's
summer deck, radiated past them into
the foggy chasm's depth. There, shifting
crosswinds cast brief kaleidoscopic rainbows
through folds of mist below. Olsta stood and
faced Asara, and then Tol, watching them
with eyes that said that she refused to speak.
Asara read in Olsta's face a sense
of deep concern when she looked up at Tol.
"We have become," said Tol, "much like the
moon of Attatrul upon whose broken circle
now we sit; for this is not our world;
and through extreme and strange destructions

are we here. Your planetlord, good Olsta,
shall not again extend his guiding hand
on our fair world; for it is now no more,
having in one moment lost its substance
like a bubble made of soap. I have seen
Parinmawada, wise and noble Kowd;
and of all its sober news, the gravest
is that mortality, the mark of all
the lower species, has in some places
come to touch us all—or come again—
for death dwells in the past of us who live,
or so it says. Yet worse than all of this
concern, is that I do not now accept,
as true, the truth of what appears as true;
and nothing do I trust outside of me."

Tol's eyes met those of Olsta, and he missed
Asara's anxious, troubled look. He felt
he should not tell of Ito's words and of
his wonderment about her mission from
the Source. If she and all she said were but
illusion and untruth, then what could be
the merit in retelling? But if she
spoke the truth, defiance of her once had wiped
his silver planet from the sky; and telling
secrets, Ito had said, would send still
more to ruin. Tol sighed, but said no more.

"I cannot help but feel that what you say
affects your love for me," Asara said.

"Remember that you have come here by sure
direction of the Source. Your friend, the Kowd,
by no coincidence has told you things
that he himself just learned; and those are thoughts
which, like the image of our world destroyed
and all its Beings gone we know not where,
is every way impossible to think.
Turn not your thoughts within yourself, dear Tol,
nor think of me. Instead, go see the Kowd."

As if on cue, the pador Videvis
appeared. She looked at each of them and smiled
and asked Asara how she felt. She gave
to Tol a one-page letter penned by Ilka
Planetlord, who hoped that all was well.
With no more words, the Tersai and two Humans
took the pador's lead and went outside.
A carriage bird, which Videvis had called,
soon lifted them to clouded heights above
the empty halls of Ilka's summer home.
Hot, moist air rose to enfold them from a
forest's leafy denseness. The bird was soon
descending, in a circle, down to where
the evening's shadows marked a gap among
the trees. Around the edges of this large
and isolated aperture, a thick
green flood of flowered vines drained quickly into
shade. It was through here the bird soared down
and left its cargo on the forest floor.

The pador said to wait awhile, ran off,
and soon came back—her motionless commander,
Kowd Parinmawada, in her arms.

"My pador tells me that my visitor
himself is now a host," the limbless Being
smiling spoke to those it could not see.

"I am here, with Olsta," Asara said,
"and we have heard from Tol, since we have come,
about your learned research of the Higher
Species' past, about death, about speaking
words that are not true, and all about
your chill conclusion that we all once shared
the grim despairing fate of lower beings.
Our silver world, you know by now, is gone.
The Tersai on it have been blasted further
than they may be found; and all the Kowd
and Humans, even if they may be found,
might not—we do not know—be remade whole
by gravity and Craft. On top of this,
you say that death has recommenced in Stellar
Sector Five. I feel my spirit ache,
and Tol tells me that this was once called fear.
Have you some news? Do you know what to do?"

The little Being did not seem disturbed
and talked in calming tones. "When I last spoke
with Tol, it seemed to us that nothing could
be done without oracular direction
from the Source. Since then, I've planned to go.

For me, the trip along the radius
of all known space will be a double duty:
first, you three and Videvis and I
shall seek all answers and an end to present
fear. Then, for me, I can complete at Centra
what you have, yourselves, accomplished many
thousand years ago—the eating of
the fabled Leaves of Love that grow next to
the Source itself. This pilgrimage, for me,
is overdue. Put by your fear for now,
and come with me to dream the starbeam's sleep."

They all agreed; and after they had clattered
over trails of aging wood, they sent
themselves, as particles of light, through space.

The Pronouncement

Chapter 6

The Pronouncement

In solemn rows and winding columns marched
the Overlords. Each from the Centran home
where he or she or it took rest, they came,
hundreds after dozens, thousands after them,
pacing gravely through the wide and level
streets that formed the City of the Source.
In weave or cut or color of their clothes,
no two were dressed alike. The Tersai Lords
bore in their muscled arms the helpless Kowd,
while Humans bore computer scrolls containing
the millennia of records which
the Council of the Overlords had kept.

From windows, and from doors, the eyes of
Centra watched the pacing urgency go by
in numbers which not one had ever seen.

The Lords require, observers thought, convening
of the total Council—rare enough
was that—and with a prohibition of
attendance through efficient and near-
palpable transmissions of the hologram.
This secret business of the Council frosted
all their faces with a concentrated
silence, as they, the watchers, listened to
the random shuffling of those many feet.

Their destination was the Council Hall,
a solemn place of spired vastness and
of fame. There, from within its glowing walls
of soft translucent stone, the laws of all
the universe were made, its projects planned,
its leaders picked, and all its business done.
Its lofty outlines, above the city,
formed of light a spiked and ornate mesa,
a place which symbolized, for Beings throughout
space, performance of the dictates of
the Source, whose greatness, thus, reached its effect
and touched and formed the universal life.

The many came, and entered, and sat down
upon its cushioned seats, which rose in tiers
made square around the level place from which
the Moderators spoke. Their office, by
solemn edict of the Source, could only be
discharged by Oracular Attendants.
Bells and clangers, cymbals and spreading gongs

were in succession sounded to assemble,
one by one, the many groups of Lords
according to their species and their
origin in space. A thousand padors, dressed
in garb of the most somber ceremony,
made show of pushing hard to shut the massive
doors of chiselled slate ten times their height,
which moved, in fact, by hidden engines' force.
All Attendants of the Source were there, all
but for Ti Rathu, Ito and I La,
who for some several thousand Centrayears
had journeyed to the Planet of the
Silver Streams upon a mission from the Source.
The six who had remained put to their lips
the coiled Horns of Centra, blasting hard
familiar strident notes that called for
order, and reflection, and debate as how
to implement oracular desire.

The six Attendants, then, as Moderators
of the Council, spoke in unison
these well-worn words: "Hear this from the Great Source,
you Overlords, '*Assemble now collective*
thought, as Beings long entrusted to
interpret all my words and will. In this
and everything, let Centra rule all space!'"

No cheers of habit followed in the Hall,
and echoes of the chanting soon dispersed.
Light angled through the prisms which were

windows in that place, and colors changed and brightened as the sun crept upwards through the sky.

"But is there yet pronouncement from the Source?" a Tersai Lord cried out at last; and soon the Council Hall was deaf with noise of other Lords beseeching this same point—and asking whether the Attendants had some news.

"My Lords," spoke one Attendant in an effort to be heard, "there have been no words at all
from our Great and Universal Source
since that strange day, long past, when three of us
Attendants were, by the Source, dispatched to go
through space from which they've not returned.
No dance, nor incantation, nor appeal,
which we Attendants have each hour, each day,
made patiently within oracular
domain, has brought result. For all these many
thousand Centrayears, it is as if
the Source's voice went with our fellows three."

"There has been error or mistake!" a Human Lord was heard to shout. Then, from confusion of their many voices, rhythmic chanting pulsed into possession of the Hall:

"Petition! Petition! Withdraw the old!
Advance one new! Petition! Petition!"
The Council's shouts grew louder with each word
until, at last, a Kowd named El, borne in
a pador's arms, took its position on

the dais; and, when all the chanting ceased,
it raised its voice and spoke out to the throng.

"It has been five and forty hundred thousand
years since I made motion, to these Lords,
for purpose of petitioning the Source.
Proposing the Petition of All Time,
I spoke, in this same Hall, of history
which most had long forgot—the Abolitions,
First and Second, and wide skeins of time
unravelling the Ages: first, of War,
then Art, then Pilgrimage, and last came Love.
I drew for you, in words, a picture of
the grand achievement of our noble kind—
how we took space and filled it with the beauty
of new worlds, and having then created
space, and made it good, how we then were
made recreated by consumption of
those leaves, the taste of which made pilgrims learn
to love. Our history, I said, and you
agreed, had risen though its stages like
a bird in mounting flight, until it hung
relaxed upon the perfect soaring breeze
and should, by present edict of the Source,
be made a thing of permanence in time.

"Thus, I proposed this chamber should approach
the Oracle and make petition for
the abolition of all change. By this,
acknowledged in these few debating years,

our freedoms stand to be enhanced, unshouldered
from the duty and the care which we,
all bound in time, take on ourselves to make,
or seem to make, our history advance.
The implement of history should thus be
fulfilled and, now grown old and useless, ended.
We were resolved, on this my motion to
the Lords, that we the Higher Species have,
in fact, in our lengthy journey, found
a sheltered clearing of repose, in which
the dewy softnesses of love give such
unequallable delights that further
foresting in time could not a better make."

"The plague! The plague!" The darkened clouds
of noise burst down upon the dream rehearsed by El.
"Withdraw and take back this petition, now!"
El heard these words but whispered to its pador
that it wished to speak no more. It left
the stage with its petition unwithdrawn.

Then one Attendant raised her Human voice
above the fray. "I am Ra Thon and have,
these centuries, made full devotion to
the tending of the words which are the Source.
I and my fellows chant and sing each day
unceasingly to pass along what you,
the Overlords, resolve to ask the Source.
It is on us that, when the Source does speak,
blind trances—passing sleep—descend and make

us very still, as half of us are made
to speak, in unison, those words beyond
ourselves, which as we speak we cannot hear.
The other half take care to listen and
to certify, to this great Hall, these words.
Be you all assured that we have told the Source
of your concerns. Heed, all of you, the rule
that says 'Be patient of your hearing of the Source.'"

Ra Thon then stood aside as there arose
Uskeete, the Planetlord of Centra and
a Kowd of high regard. "Good Lords," it spoke,
"where there are no choices, there cannot be
debate. Who can recall when we have faced
such mysteries? First, we were told that death
and sickness had appeared in Higher Species
throughout Stellar Sector Five. Second,
when we had quarantined these stars so that
disease, and news of it, would be contained,
we were convened by three Attendants of
the Source: Ito, I La and Ti Rathu,
whose message from the Oracle was that
those three should span known space and bring back
here an Aliadni, from the Planet of
the Silver Streams, who was, by that world's wisest,
deemed to be most learned in the Way
of Life. Now, ten score of millennia,
as measured by this planet's sun, have passed
from when those three, made Envoys by this House,

departed by the will of our Great Source.
Now the time has surely come for their return,
and now may come the news we need to hear."

Its words gave way to padors' steps that ran
towards the stage, bearing an urgent message
taken from the signals of deep space.
Ra Thon took it and read: "'All greetings from
this Silver World,' it says, 'and hail to the
Great Source. Know that your envoys soon depart,
and with them, Bal, our planet's sovereign Lord.
May joy be yours, as Centra rules all space.'"

Ra Thon looked up from what she read and said,
"Good Lords, Uskeete has spoken like a rain
in spring which has sent out a promise of
new tender shoots of growth—those words from space—
which not too soon may flower to our needs."

But then a Human Lord, one of the several
Keepers of the Scrolls, raised up his voice:
"Make still, for now, your murmuring of hope.
Be not assured that certainty arrives.
My scrolls, which yet preserve what memory
has lost, tell me that Bal, the Planetlord,
had life after the Great Abolition
of Death and so is no Aliadni;
and thus the Envoys bring not what they sought."

A motion followed that they should adjourn
and take their rest, at home, until the news
another day would bring—but this the Lords

refused. The last pronouncement from the Source had been direction that the envoys pierce deep space; and now, with their returning close at hand, the Lords remained in silent vigil, pending revelation of new truth.

The tiers of rows of stone-still faces pressed all around the stage on which their expectation would arrive. Silent, too, was all of Centra in the knowledge that the Overlords were sitting through the night. The outbound Centran signals, bearing this event, had travelled but a fraction to the nearest peopled world when Centra, in its sluggish turning, slid its curving rim of night across the City of the Source.

Just when the first light of Kolku had prismed through the Hall, the beams that bore the Envoys reached the crystals of their rest. As five Attendants of the Source looked on, the beams reflected into forms that soon became I La, and Ti Rathu, and with them, Bal, the Planetlord of Silver Springs. While these three began to stir, shaking from their re-formed selves the dim millennia of nearly dreamless sleep, Attendants whispered their surprise that Ito was not there and that no news had reached them, in advance, why this third envoy was not with the rest.

Strong legs propelled a waiting cart
which sped the three directly to the stage.
The Moderators blew their horns for quiet.
Then, after she embraced the muscled form
of strong I La and stooped to hold, in welcome,
the squat and twisted form of Ti Rathu,
Ra Thon raised up her Human voice for all:
"The gravity of time has pulled two-thirds
of our expectation from suspense.
Before us are the Kowd and Tersai who,
by direct speaking of the Source, have crossed,
and then recrossed, the radius of space.
To you—and him we know as Bal—welcome.
Such are, however, our concerns that with
no glad politeness or delay we ask
you now: why have you brought Bal Planetlord,
whom records show had life in time well past
the ancient Age of the Aliadni?
And where is the third Envoy of the three,
the Human, Ito, of such beauty and
renown? Why did the signals from the world
of silver springs confirm she'd be with you?"

"I know I speak," I La replied in rapid
tones, "for Ti Rathu, as well, when I
tell you that we three envoys took with us
who we were told was nominated, by
the Council of the Wisest, as that
Aliadni, of that world, most learned in

the Way of Life; and equally impossible
is that we left together, three
Envoys and this Bal, yet have arrived
without fair Ito or the knowledge where
she is. By this, I am most strangely startled
from these many years of deepest sleep."

Ra Thon began to make reply, but she
was interrupted then by Bal, who spoke:
"Good Overlords and fellow planetlord,
Uskeete, please now accept, in place of the
expression of my humblest great respects,
my strong assurance, to you, that the answers
to the questions of Ra Thon will come
from the Envoy Ito herself, who, for
reasons which I venture not explain,
holds special insight into your concerns."

"Good Planetlord," Uskeete replied, "do not
withhold your thoughts. We seek the answers to
much larger problems than you are aware."

To this, the planetlord was slow to give
reply. At length, he said, "From Ito, I
believe I am here by Oracular
demand. For more than that, you must ask her."

"For more than that I make demand of you!"
Uskeete retorted, with approval murmured
sternly all around. "Tell what you know,
and tell us now, as Centra rules all space."

Bal turned pale to see such expectation
fire in the eyes of power and of fame.
"My Lords," he said, "I tremble to refuse
the thing you ask. To do so, I invoke,
of the constating rules by which this House
holds reign, that one which says a planetlord
may make appeal, to the Great Source itself,
of a directive from this House, which but
for this my right, would otherwise be law."

Whatever Bal may have expected from
the Overlords, he did not think they would
respond with long and unrestrained applause.
"Be not amazed," Ra Thon spoke up, "that your
refusal and appeal, good Bal, brings to
the Lords such joy. For reasons you know not,
this House has for too many centuries
been seeking some pronouncement from the Source,
but there has been none. Now, my heart leaps up
with your assertion of constating right.
We need wait no more. Now, the Source must speak!"

"The Source must speak! The Source must speak!"
The Lords took up the chanted cry and crowded
down the aisles of the Hall to follow out
behind Ra Thon and all Attendants, who
proceeded onwards to the Source. Outside
the Hall, the Beings of the City cleared
a path for this so fast and loud parade

which flooded through the level boulevard,
extending to the Oracle itself.

The Oracle existed at a place,
and that place was called Enigma. Located
at the center of the City of the Source,
its dark glass dome gave no reflection
to the sky, nor to the arching colored
fountains lanced with lasered fire, which formed
in rows the setting for this pearl of jet.
Inside, one-half of the Attendants had
been chanted to a trance and sat, transfixed,
in expectation of a voice that used
no words. The other half stood poised to make
transcription of what those entranced would speak.

Outside, the crowds of Lords and others sat
and stood and waited for some happening
within. When some time passed and night had come,
the fountains started pumping higher than
before; and this, all knew, meant that the Source
would speak. Yet, waiting lingered into days,
and many took their rest at home and wondered
there when they would learn of Bal's appeal.

Then came the quiet of a cloudy dawn
in which the fountains leapt their highest arc.
With one small nod, Ra Thon made known the Lords
should come; and in the Hall, when all were there,
she handed to I La a tiny scroll.
I La stood and spoke, "I am honored now

to read, as you to hear, this, of the Source:
'*Lords of Centra, give pause and hear your news....*'"

Just as I La pronounced these words, a pador
from the signal screens raced down the steps
and tossed towards I La another scroll.
He picked it up and read, "'From Attatrul,
to all who dwell in space: know that our neighbor
planet, full of silver streams, has burst
apart, disframing into vapors and
small bits. But for some fading hope we can
retrieve some Tersai from the void, the only
counsel of our Ilka, Planetlord,
is to reflect and wait to hear the Source.
Hear this, our news, as Centra rules all space.'"

Uskeete was first to gather breath for words:
"There need not be pronouncing of this change
of law: these words betide repeal of
abolition of calamity in nature,
that firm foundation stone of our lives,
pronounced to us when first the Source did speak."

"The Source has spoken more," rejoined I La
and lifted up his scroll, '*Lord Bal's appeal
is granted, for already has there been
a true pronouncement made, and it was to
a single Being, who shall tell you all.*'"

The Mirror

Chapter 7

The Mirror

"So many worlds we Higher Species build;
so many stars have beckoned us to roam;
so full is all our joy in what we do,
and fuller still the love that binds us all.
So empty is our memory of those
events which long eroding time has worn;
so few of founding minutes withstand years;
not one cool tile, in the floors we tread,
reminds us with what heat it once was fired."

In words as these, Attendant Ito spoke
her thoughts, addressing her sole self as she
appeared reflected in a mirror's frame.
She had awakened back on Centra, where,
without announcement, and on learning what
events were then distracting all the planet

and its Lords, she quietly retreated
to her home; and here she asked the mirrored
image to review, and to consider,
and, if possible, then, to explain
the feelings she had come to know as fear.

"Not only, then," Ito went on, "have we,
the Higher Species, we of greater minds,
so long forgotten all our paths that new
reminding seems like unknown ground; but also,
I, respected noble and Attendant
of the Source, have been so long applied
in service to its words that I forgot
what still is recent in the history
of space: what joy there is in love. Then this
Tol finds my heart, this Human twists my soul;
and I, seeking power, find only love,
then, seeking love, lie in the dust of his
refusal. I and confusion are one."

A steady chiming pushed away her thoughts
and told her of some business at her door.
She soon was taking from a pador's hand
a message, when unscrolled, revealed to her
the Overlords had learned she had arrived
and that they sought her presence at the Hall.

"I cannot speak," she said, returning to
the glass, "before the Lords, of what weighs down
my heart; and so to you, O clearest image
of myself, I shall confess and make

review and shall command that you will stand
in strict attention to my every word."
She smiled a smile of weariness and thought.
Outside, the pador waited her reply
and through her garden dodged and played with
squirrels, chipmunks and some gentle nut-brown mice
that burrowed in the ground behind her home.

"You know it was no special day Ra Thon
and I passed through Enigma's polished doors,
to sit and contemplate the silence of
the Source. The plague wore on and worsened
out in Stellar Sector Five, unknown to all
except its victims and us Lords. These
silences became for us, through centuries,
a way of life. No sooner had Ra Thon
sat down than she began, from deep within
a wooden trance, to utter words in that
sure voice in which the Source alone can speak.

"'*Ito,*' it spoke, '*you know the Lords do now
consider the Petition of All Time.
In this they seek the abolition of
all change - the crystallizing of perfection
in the present Age of Love. This shall
be granted, but not as any would expect.
A universe advanced beyond all change
shall be governed, not by a hall of Lords
instructed by the Source, but rather by
a monarch, a single Higher Being*

who embodies power throughout space.
Know that this Higher Being shall be you.'

"The lazy star, Kolku, that gives to Centra
heat, moves back and forth through its galactic
cycle in more years than one has time
to count. I served the Source and fellow Lords
through more such cycles than there are known stars.
Eighty-three words from the Source, and I felt
I never lived and never had been born."

Then turning from the glass, she pressed her
face into her hands. Like unseen silver mists
appearing into pools that brimmed, and dropped, from
tips of purple ferns throughout the world that was
no more, tears came and sprinkled to the floor.
In tones unheard since long before she had,
through force applied by Aliadni Craft,
been given life, she sobbed and cried and wept
until her anguish soaked her feet and all
her misery had filled the hollow room.

Her breath came back, and she could speak
again: "I studied the fixated face of good
Ra Thon, my friend; but speaking for the Source,
she could, of course, hear nothing that she said
nor could she hear my words. I overcame
a draining dizziness and then spoke to
the Source: 'As Centra rules all space,
what Being could so rule instead, and which
of any Higher Species, if myself

or any other, could so share the power
that defines the Great and Universal Source?'

"'*You shall not share the rule of space; and when
you rule, the Universal Source shall cease.
Do you decline to do what is pronounced*?'
The Source thus spoke, and I felt a sudden
weakness bloating me, with heaviness
of sand, and dulling me from all sensation
but that of my immobility.
In all time forward from that point, I have
not felt my mind or life to be my own;
and all my words—to others, self-spoken,
or said in dreams—have been but ghostly
resonances of the Source's unreal words.

"'*Again, Ito,*' the Oracle continued,
'*Do you decline or do you now accept*?'

"'Please, how may I, Great Source, accept a
station of such unattainable honor,
and worthiness, not having worth or honor
equal to the task of treading servant
worlds as the embodiment of power
without check, whose will is law, whose
judgment finality and whose fancy fact?
And more than that, how may the governance
of space—for order, peace, stability,
sure planning and for love—be carried out
except by all sure dictates of the Source?'

"'*The Source's dictate is that you obey.*
Once more, and once more only, do you now
accept the rule of space? Say yes, or go.'

"'As Centra rules all space,' I said at length,
'I shall do what the Source commands of me.'

"'*Hear, then, what you must know. A monarch*
rules upon foundations built of what you soon
shall know as falsehood. Power flows from myth.
Myth comes from common error in assessment
of events defining what is real.
You shall induce such error and rule space.
In Stellar Sector Five, there comes now death.
You shall declare, before the Lords, that they
must send a certain Higher Being to
the place where death has come; and he and all
among those stars shall die; but, thereafter,
death shall spread no more; and your rule shall be
justified; and this shall be the last event
before the Abolition of All Change.'

"What could have been," asked Ito of her
other self, "a further reasoned answer to
the Source? Could I have made an argument
the Oracle was wrong? Could I have said
my station was too far below where I
was told to be—or that I could not do
what I was told I could? Or then could I,
unworthy, find unworthiness in me
where worthiness had, by the Source, been found?

I told the Source that I would rule all space.
I promised to be careful in deceit.
I said I would do nothing but in
furtherance of myths of power, outlasting change.
The Source explained the strangeness of deceit.
The Source did not reveal a future drenched in tears.

"'What need I know,' I asked the Source,
'beyond what you have said, to bring all this to pass?'

"'*Three things: first, you shall have ability,*
personal to you, to seem to be a
Being other than yourself; second, you
shall be able to project false images
into another's mind; and third, you
shall be able to bring about, by Craft,
destruction of a planet when its end
shall suit your pattern of deceit; for this....'

"I was then as enraptured as Ra Thon
and so was startled at that moment when
I La, and with him Ti Rathu, came
interrupting the instructions of the Source;
but then as if the Source knew not those two
had come, its voice continued with its words.

"'*...for this, and most important to the task,*
you must now go retrieve, upon the Planet
of the Silver Streams, that Aliadni
who, according to that Planet's Council
of the Wise, appears most deeply learned

in the Way of Life. Hear this and go.'
Concluding silence followed, then, throughout.
"'What is "the task?"' I La inquired,
setting down the limbless Kowd upon a stool
and sitting down, himself, next to Ra Thon.
'How comes pronouncement with no fountain's sure
display, and what was said before we came?'
"Nothing! Nothing! Nothing!" Ito shook her
fist before the mirror to recall that
day within Enigma's dome. "Nothing can
explain the why and how of what I said
to good I La, as my dear friend, Ra Thon,
shook off her dreams in eagerness to hear
what solemn words of greatness she had said
while speaking for the Source; and nothing can
restore the sand that scattered in that hour
from the broken glass of time; and nothing
can be said to any Higher Being
of the words and deeds which place myself—
in all relation to all else—behind
a mirror's glass and give all three dimensions
to a passable reflection, which
all other Beings think is really me.
"'Good Ti Rathu, O learned Kowd,' thus I
began my sampling of deceit, 'and you,
I La, and my Ra Thon, who never tires
of my tea, the Source, strange though it sound,
had need to speak in private, through Ra Thon,

to us, the other three. The Source declared
a task, the first of which was simply that
I wait for both of you. The second part
you heard, that we, the three of us who heard
these words, should travel on a quest through space.'

"'Though private in its making,' uttered Ti
Rathu, responding to my lie, 'this new
pronouncement, long awaited and so much
desired, must now be placed before the Lords.'

"The Lords, of course," Ito recalled, "took all
of this to mean a path had cleared toward
the ending of the plague. When I, and the
two other envoys, as we had been duly
and with ceremony made, stood waiting
on the crystal stage to nod into
the starbeam's lightspeed nap, I planned a plan
to get the power which was mine to get.

"The scheme was that I should persuade the
silver planet's lord, whose name was Bal, to hide
from view the choice made by the wise so that
I could retrieve him, later, on my own
and that way give myself all credit for
securing Tol and his deliverance.
I considered that I spoke the truth when I
told Bal the Oracle demanded that
he lie; and when, by force of what I said,
he came with me and left his voiceless mate,

I felt a thrilling shudder in my loins
as if new power worked on me as love.

"As Bal, the other Envoys and myself
prepared to leave that silver world, I gave
a strict command to one small pador that
the starbeam should be split and that I be
deflected to the planet's southmost place,
thus leaving those three others Centrabound.
The beast gave its unthinking bond of silence;
and it carried out the shifting of
such crystals as accomplished my escape;
and to the home of Tol the Hermit then I came.

"I searched all day amidst volcanic dust
and silver fog and found no Tol; but one
level and open place, among the mountains
near a cave, gave rest to what remained
of crystals wrought of Craft unknown to me;
and there, in silence wrung from thought, I heard
the mountains echo words which late had struck
those slopes with power that could keep their sense
alive; and I heard this: '*...to Attatrul...*
to Attatrul....' So, half aimless and half
believing that, thus wandering, I did
the Source's will, to Attatrul I went.

"Once there, I was renewed to find how
easily I could, by falsehood, keep concealed
my purpose and my name. I learned, in
simple conversation, an arrival from

their silver neighbour had, by carriage bird,
just lifted off towards the Crater Krel.
I followed there, and I concealed myself
in dust and barren stones where none would think,
if any thought, to look. Thus hid, I heard
the Kowd Parinmawada speak as if
it had been privy to the Lords, and to
the Source, and to myself—so much it seemed
to know. It spoke to Tol, the object of
my stealthful hunt. Tol and the Kowd then parted,
and I followed Tol up to the famous
Chasm of Logall; but, deeper than
that gorge which stabs into the sea, was the
division which I found within myself.

"I had not thought of what the Source had said
except as dictates which must be obeyed;
but as I from a distance watched this Tol
and listened to his idle speaking to
the padors, to the passing birds, and to
the stars, and as I saw a graceful strength
in both his movements and his words,
I realized that I resolved to do,
in planning to dispatch him to his death,
the thing of horror which the Kowd described:
murder, the last removal of a life
from consciousness; and the words of the Source
were both duty and fate, for me as final
as the end of Tol would be. Nothing,

then, could confuse me more than that I fell
in love with Tol, and more and more I felt
this love as I made study of my prey.

"I cannot say how love like this took root,
or how it stirred my heart, despite my
overhearing Tol's lament of every foot
of distance from a Tersai love he called
Asara. I am witness, though, as I
observe my heart, of that so strange and sad
impossibility, that I should love,
when he and I had never met and he,
whom I loved more and more, loved someone else.

"As twisting gusts of cold and misty air
came gasping from the chasm's hollow throat,
I sat and thought and shook, within my hidden
vantage, fearful—in Parinmawada's
word—of what new feeling tunnelled, wormlike,
in my heart and made me wish for harm
to come to her he loved or, failing that,
for me, somehow or other, to be her.

"What followed was the purest of events.
By force of what had hold of me, what then
occurred, while happening, revealed no taint
or stamp or certain mark of my free will.
O mirror! When I glanced down into a small
protected pool of recent rain and saw
your liquid cousin shining back a Being
not myself, that moment was the end

of what, before the Lords, I should be made
to make account, as servant to the Source.

"I clutched and pulled my face, and still I was
not me. I stripped my gown and found, beneath,
much darker skin, wider hips, larger breasts,
and longer legs, above which bright blond hairs
conveyed this change of mine was quite complete."

Thinking this, Ito laughed a bit and stepped
away from where her mirror stood. She paused
and smoothed her hair; and then she sat and looked
out of her window at the tidy street
of houses where her neighbors long had lived.
The pador which the Lords had sent was playing
with a giant cat, racing in circles
on her lawn and tumbling on her flowers.

"It was surprising," she continued, in
a lower tone of voice, "how my concern—
that my famed beauty had been lost—gave way
to joy that what the Source had said now came
to pass. By thinking I would be another,
I was she; and as Asara, I
was loved. With such exhilaration did
I lift a jagged stone to crush it with
Asara's Tersai strength that now was mine!
By such device, I thought, a monarch fills
desire, ruling all reality in space;
but as I thought and pressed upon the stone,

it did not yield or break. Despite the person
whom I seemed, I had but Human strength.

"I went to Tol, and I told him in words
that barely seemed my own that I was
Asara. At first, his eyes confirmed his love;
but in my arms, it melted like hot snow.
Just as he stepped away, however, all
confusion yielded to sweet clarity;
and I could see that Tol should know that thing
called fear, and would, so knowing, come with me.
I thought an image of his planet's end,
and saw, just as the Source had said, that this
projected to his mind, as on some
inner screen. Yet fear did not prevail to make
him show his love, and so I thought some more.

"My love for Tol had made me think that I
would share with him the rule of space; but when
I offered this, and he refused, I squarely
faced that I felt love for one who must
soon die. Remembering that I had left,
upon his planet, Beings who, when asked,
could bring to light the falsehood wrought with Bal,
I then effected silence, from them, and—
I hoped—from Tol, by one quick, easy act:
destruction of his silver world, together
with a promise that more worlds would meet
their end if Tol should say what I had said.

What next to do, I then resolved, could only
follow my awakening at home.
"As Centra rules all space, how can I be
responsible that falsehood proved its force
with Bal and not with Tol? As I was acting
on direction of the Source, can I
be held to have defied direction by
my failing to retrieve him, as was planned;
or if eruption of my heart has
intervened, can love be disobedient?
And, most important, should this plan of falsehood,
having now not worked, be set aside
in favor of my telling all the Lords
of what has been and how it has occurred?
Or has, regardless, absence of this
Aliadni brought about the permanence
of death in Sector Five, or even throughout space?
And has my love for him made this occur?"
As Ito left her house towards the Council
of the Lords, she noticed that the pador
had inscribed, in dirt among her flowers
then in freshest bloom, the letter V.

The Deception

Chapter 8

The Deception

Warbling birds had abandoned cover from
a recent rain; and having fatted on
unlucky worms, they flapped and waddled in
a feathered ring atop a jewelled tower,
soiling the ledge of the crystal bowl, which,
on Centra, brought to rest all starbeams from
deep space. Parinmawada, Tol, Asara,
Olsta and the pador, Videvis,
came to the end of slumbered trails of time;
and when the crystals flashed acceptance of
their dim transmitted selves, the birds flew off
and sought the peacefulness of other heights.

The travellers, when they had gathered their
awareness that to Centra they had come,
strolled off to wander in a park. The sculpted

land rolled miles through the City of
the Source. Here, fish of varied colors swam
in ponds and creeks which brimmed with many waters
from where life had reached in space, and massive
blue and orange fungi tilted domes
of shade on passers-by along the mossed
and lilied water's edge. They walked, at first,
in silence, marvelling at quiet
unconcern, and smiling peacefulness, that marked
the faces of the Higher Beings in
the park. From this, they knew the Lords concealed
the outbreak of the terror, known as death,
and that the planet Centra had not learned,
from anyone, their silver planet's end.

"Since I am here as pilgrim," spoke the Kowd
from where it nestled in Asara's arms,
"I ask your kind transporting to the trees
around the Source. There, I shall put an end
to long anticipation of those blooms
which generate awakenings in all."

"Nothing keeps us from Enigma," said
Asara, "but the beauty of this park, which
you will never see but which, from all of us,
will soon slip under shades of moonless night.
The universe, while we slept along its length,
has grown older by so many million
Centradays that our approaching of
the Lords can surely wait the morning's light.

So let us now, before Kolku has set,
approach the Source, so you may eat its leaves.
Let Tol walk in his revery. Let Olsta,
speechless still but thinking what to say
when she sees Bal, come hand in hand with me."

The grove of Centratrees had, since the Age
of Art, stood open to the traffic of
all pilgrims to that place; but now there stood
a fence around the trees; and at its gate,
a soft-eyed Tersai male addressed them thus:

"No matter what the distance you have come,
be not inclined to make your pilgrimage
of flowers. The Overlords, by special edict,
fenced the trees. They placed me here to warn
that eating of the leaves is now believed
to bring, to all, a consequence so
undesired that all pilgrimage should cease."

"What is that consequence," the tiny Kowd
inquired, "and who last ate the Leaves of Love?"

"The Lords have not revealed what follows from
their eating, and the last to eat the leaves
were pilgrim Beings here from Stellar Sector
Five. They left. Since then, the latest signals
from those stars originated prior
to their date of due return back home."

The Kowd then asked the Tersai guard, "Do you
here speak but caution, or do you prohibit,
for the Lords, that which you have cautioned?"

The guard closed both his eyes and laughed a
mighty laugh. "What Higher Being in all space,"
he asked, when laughter yielded to his words,
"would not be ruled by caution from the Lords?"

"I, myself, wish notwithstanding, now, to eat
those leaves." At this, Asara glanced at Tol
and took Parinmawada to one side.

"The last to eat the leaves were first to die,"
she spoke in urgent whispers to the Kowd,
"and you appear impatient to be next.
Do you now seek to share the rotting death
of lower species and to live no more?"

When it appeared the Kowd would not respond,
Tol answered her and said, "The mysteries
connecting all the knowledge of the Kowd
cannot be understood by those of us,
like you and me, who are divided and
distracted by our sex and by our sight.
If it will eat the leaves, then I believe
that we should give assistance to that end."

The pador, Videvis, they barely noticed,
had gone missing and was not a part
of their procession, which, astonishing
the guard, invaded paths grown over with
deliberate neglect and brought the hungry
Kowd among the fabled blooms. It ate
and smiled, in strange peacefulness, when done.

The travellers retired to the food
and drink and stationary sleep which seemed,
to ask the keeper of their inn, as overdue.
The day that followed barely seemed
to dawn, as puffs of wet black fog, drifting
over city streets, painting darkness where
it went, prevented all activity
until it yielded to a dull mid-morning
haze. Parinmawada showed no ill
effect, or any change at all, from eating
Leaves of Love; but it was very quiet,
in Asara's steady arms, as it
and its one Tersai and two Human friends
approached, in thinning fog, the Council Hall.

Outside the Hall, the speechless Olsta pointed,
wide-eyed, at a Tersai whom she
recognized to be I La, Attendant of
the Source, last seen departing with her husband,
Bal. I La approached the group and spoke:

"I know you, Olsta, member of the Council
of the Wise on that fair world where late
your husband ruled as Lord. I am I La,
Attendant, Envoy and one time a guest
of yours. Without my saying why, I hope
these friends with you are also of your world."

"Tol is my name," said Tol, responding for
his muted friend, "much less well known from where
the silver waters ran before our planet

lit the distant skies, burning, its ashes
then dissolving clear into the liquid
of the night. Do you, Attendant, know
of what, in history, was once called grief?"

"Your words," I La replied to Tol, "unloose
in me a flood of thoughts and questions which
might unconfine the pressure which has numbed
me from duty and all use. Yet tell
me more of you and why you all are here."

"Asara, here, and I have come to seek
opinion of the Lords about our planet's
end. The Kowd, Parinmawada, is
a pilgrim, reflecting now upon its
recent tasting of the Leaves of Love; and Olsta,
also of the silver world that is no more,
can speak no words but, with her eyes, tells us
she seeks her husband, known to you as Bal,
your other host and, of our planet, Lord."

Some moments passed, and then I La directed
them to sit upon the steps outside
the Council Hall, and he began to speak.

"I wonder if it is by random chance
alone that we have met, so much is my
confusion matched with yours. I have just now
been speaking with a Tersai, named Valkav,
who tells a story which, although repeated
twice, almost persuades me I have been
mistaken in my hearing. You, good Olsta,

know whom you and others of the wisest
chose to join us envoys, Centrabound.
Yet, could you know, as well, that he you chose
is not the Being who returned with us?
"Valkav escaped dispersion into
nothingness, the general fate of Tersai of
your world, when, on explosion, his strong body
struck, by chance too small for thought, one of
your planet's moons. He came directly here
to me and says that he was also of
your wisdom's group, on your far world where silver
waters flowed, and that you, Olsta, bore
the secret scroll to Ito and to Bal
whereon it was inscribed that we would bring
a certain hermit, living in your planet's
frigid south, and not Bal Planetlord,
whom Ito and your Bal declared to all
to be the choice. That hermit's name," he said,
turning to speak to Tol, "was just as yours:
Tol. Are you, then, the one who should have come?"
"I do not know," said Tol, "of what the Tersai,
Valkav, in his wisdom, speaks; and Olsta
yet endures unhelpful silence. I,
in meditation during time in which
the universe grew old, drew no conclusion
lightly, and I shall not do so now.
Instead, I beg you, bring us now before the Lords."

"Yes, do come with me into the Hall, where I
shall place before the Lords apparent speaking
of what is not true," replied I La.
They followed up the steps and then inside.

When all assembled and the doors were closed
and all the Horns of Centra put aside,
the Lords' attention fixed upon the strangers
whom I La insisted should be there.
Then, silhouetted by the solid gray
of one vast door, and motionless against
its bulk, the lonely form of Ito sent
increasing waves of noisy recognition
through the seats; and all the Lords rejoiced
that this long-sought Attendant had returned.
They watched Bal Planetlord and Olsta weep
in long embrace to end their time apart.
They also saw the puzzlement with which
Asara viewed the steady and unblinking
gaze exchanged between Ito and her Tol.

Uskeete, the planetlord of Centra, sensed,
as sometimes sense the Kowd, that long-sought
information would that day emerge, and to
the Hall, it spoke: "Lords, and those Beings who
are strangers to this place, hear me and tell,
those who may know, if any here have had—
or know of such—pronouncement of the Source
unknown as yet to us, the Overlords.
A single Higher Being, as the Source

last said, has earlier received the Source's
words; and we believe such words will answer
questions which, for far too many thousand
years, have filled our days and nights with grave
concern and ended lives on distant worlds.
Speak to us now, as Centra rules all space!"

With reluctance and what used to be called
dismay, two Humans, male and female, stepped
towards the dais where the sexless Kowd
had spoken. Ito, from one side, and Tol,
from where he stood across, made way through whispers
which, when they had reached Uskeete, increased
to noisy shouts of "Hear them speak! Now speak!"

"Hear me!" yelled Tol, and quiet followed soon.
"Good Lords, I am unknown to you, but this
is so for reasons which I leave to Bal,
my former planet's Lord, to justify
to you. Long contemplation gave me Craft
to hear the Source directly on my world;
and thinking that the mystery of Bal's
departure justified my breach of his
command, I used this Craft and heard the Source
tell me, Asara here as witness, the
Petition is denied and that I should
depart my world and go to Attatrul.
Once there, this Kowd revealed to me the past
which has long overflowed containment in
our memories, the truth of which has been

confirmed by truth of what it also said
about the secret deaths in Sector Five.
I ask to know what this Petition is."

Tol paused amid the Lords' surprise that he
could know about the quarantine of death—
or that he knew, or thought he knew, the Source
had ruled on the Petition made by El;
but then Tol thought of Ito's words, that his
revealing that they met would finish other
worlds. Thus he resolved to speak no more just then.

Ito spoke next: "Great stars have shone and died
since I first served this Hall, attending to
the Source. Before I was made Envoy, I
received pronouncement which I La and sexless
Ti Rathu had overheard in part.
The balance, on instruction from the Source,
I concealed, but do now make known. I learned
the object of the Envoy's quest to be
this Human, Tol, and that by sending him
to dream the starbeam's sleep and go to Sector
Five, the plague shall shortly end. I also
learned that the petition, made so long
ago by El, will shortly be allowed."

A smile spread across the wizened face
of El, who had so long resisted, from
its fellow Lords, all pressure to withdraw.
"The Envoy speaks the truth," it said, in tones
that all could hear. "Not one petition, since

the Source gave words, has been denied.
No Higher Being, other than a Lord, has
ever heard the Oracle; and never has
that so great voice been heard but on the soil
of Centra! Lords! As this world rules all space,
did none of you perceive, within the Source's
words, a fine redundancy, when we
were told a single Being had received
a '*true pronouncement*'? What pronouncement is
untrue? Consider that this Tol was not
alone when he or something made him think
that he had heard the Source, and so no single
Being heard the words which came to him."

"Yet," came interruption from I La, "think
on this: that less than all of what was said
to Ito was to her alone. Then, how
but by the Oracle would Tol infer
existence of the Kowd's petitioning,
since he is not a Lord? And if, as El
suggests, this Human Tol speaks words which are
not true, what likely sense is there to send
a Being so infected, through deep space,
to Sector Five and where contagion reigns?"

"I am both witness and participant
in falsity regarding Tol," said Bal,
speaking sternly, "and I will now, if you
will hear, describe deception which, before,
I had concealed when questioned by Uskeete."

"My husband! Speak!" These were the first words Olsta spoke since rendered mute so many Centrayears ago. "Correct the error which has followed from deception from your lips!"

"Let me, instead," said Ito, "place before this Hall the full extent of the deception of this Tol. By intuition, or some other means, this Human must have learned that his deception and his disobedience to Bal, just now confessed, would bring about what has not happened within memory, save in Sector Five: namely, harm to a Higher Being. Destruction of the Planet of the Silver Streams prevents our knowing if, as I suspect, Tol learned he had been named by members of the Wise.

"He feared," continued Ito, looking straight at Bal, "if any are acquainted with that term, that harm would come to him; and he used Craft to make us Envoys think that Bal, not he, was chosen to come here. Good Bal now offers witness to this fact. Yet on oracular command, I followed Tol. On Attatrul, I planned a plan to lure him Centrabound. Now we shall send this Tol, on order of the Source whom I have served, to meet his end in Stellar Sector Five. His falsity and death shall join to make

an antidote for what has poisoned space
and brought, to us, the terror of the lower
species' fate. Let Centra rule all space!"

Without more speaking or debate or hearing
more from Bal, the Lords adjourned to think
upon what they had heard that day and whether,
as it seemed, Attendant Ito was
that Being who the Source had said would bring
a true pronouncement to their ears. They sent,
again, Attendants to Enigma, chanting
pleas for more assistance from the Source.

Near Enigma, beneath a darkened sky,
Olsta and Bal held reunited hands,
while Tol, Asara and I La sat
quietly around a seat on which the Kowd
Parinmawada made its Kowd-like squat.
When fading evening had surrendered to
the night, the sound of spraying water reached
their ears and told them, by the mounting liquid
arcs around its dome, the Source would speak.

Yet as the fountains reached their height, an odd
contortion seized Parinmawada's face.
Then, as the others watched, including several
passing Overlords, its head rolled back;
and it began to speak, in manner and
in tone, just like the Universal Source:
"*Tol must now go to Stellar Sector Five.*
Ito rules all space. The Source shall speak no more."

The Banishment

Chapter 9

The Banishment

Tol had not waited for the Overlords'
restating of the Source's clear decree.
Nor had he said good-bye to any,
even Asara; and yet, despite determined
haste, he had been met, within the crystal
place where his last travel was to start,
by Ito, who, in tears, stood in his path
and gave to him a carved and shining ring.
"Take this," she said, "and wear it as a sign
that in all things we both obey the Source
and that, in this our highest aspiration,
you and I are ever joined as one."
Tol took the ring, kissed Ito on her cheek
and stepped upon the polished deck. He looked
at her, and moments later he was gone.

His starbeam pressed, with lightspeed, through
the quietness of space. Its path, with laser straightness,
bored through spiralled galaxies and clusters,
constellations made of blue and yellow stars,
of binaries and dim, red dwarfs, and more
of purest white, then on past trails of
fleeing quasars, into tattered veils of aging
supernovas' quickspent glory, and
through nebulae that nursed a summer sky
of newborn stars before he reached his goal.

Since Sector Five lay just beyond a massive
shield of turning neutron stars, whose pulses
blocked a starbeam's path, his goal was Station K,
an empty post on a world unpeopled and
untravelled through many years of
quarantine. From here, adjacent to the neutron
shield, Tol was to dream a second sleep
and angle to his death in Sector Five.

Once regenerated and awakened,
Tol stepped outside the crystal place of his
transmission. There he saw the dust-encumbered
lounges and long lifeless gardens where
space travellers had once passed time, waiting,
as now he must, for patterns from the pulsing
stars nearby to yield a neutral gap
through which, by starbeam, one could journey on.

The station was entirely enclosed,
and sealed, against the airless void surrounding

its gray walls, its builders having seen
no need to give that world an atmosphere.
A message console glowed with recent news,
from Sector Five and sent by padors' hand,
that every Higher Being there had died.
Tol looked through a dull, pitted window at
the featureless, flat landscape and black sky
which stretched beyond; and all his thought was of
the hurt which he had brought to her he loved.

"Just as the lower species can be trained
by punishing what does not please the training
hand, my present wounding of Asara,
going from her love to certain death,
persuades me of the error, now beyond
correction, of my use of Craft to hear
the Source." So speaking, Tol cried tears that lined
his face with shining streams and, falling, made
small spots of mud upon the dusty floor.

"May she," Tol pleaded with the silence, "know
the fullness of my love for her; and as
all space evolves in Ito's rule, may she
and others know that I, whose being ceased
so as to end the plague, deserve to live
in memory, and not to end forgotten
as a tool which, in its fixing, broke.
To travel to a place, and then forget
where one has been, is to have gone nowhere.
The plague, the falsehoods, and the end of my bright

world combined concerns to make what once
was called a crisis; and that crisis stripped
the dirt which years had piled upon the carcass
of our past. Now we, whose bodies have
outlived what memories can hold, may think
upon our past to make our future real.

"Except for me!" Tol spoke with clenching fists
pressed hard against the glass. "In my sad learning
that my species once knew death, I too
shall die. I accept this. What I reject,
with all these stars as witness to my cry,
is that the Source named me the Envoys' quest
before I breached Bal's law and that, but for
such naming and the falsehood which I credit
now for Olsta's being mute, I would
have used no Craft. My life shall end for reasons
which did not exist when I was named
to die; and in this, error has ruled space."

A clicking noise proceeded from the crystal
floor where lately he had wakened to
that world. Patterns of light, racing through
angled faces of the crystal walls, leapt to
the center of the room and etched into the air
a form of Human or of Tersai shape.
Then Tol felt numb, for it was Asara.

"Greetings, my Tol," she said when she could
make full claim to consciousness. "You should not hide
your face from me, as if I did not know

and could not see that you prefer I had
not come. Now, know the worst: for far too long
I made petition of your hermit self;
and having won my suit, in your clear offer
that I join you in your quest, and having
then suggested that our partnership
commence by breaching Bal's command, I come
to you to exercise my right to share
your fate, the iron which together we have forged."

"Your right and obligation is to live,
not die," said Tol. "You were not named to share
my fate. Regardless of your sharing of
my work, regardless of our love, regardless
of what promises we made, do not
imagine that the past can justify
surrender of your future to oblivion.
That shameful path I walk alone."

"And I will let you go and will not follow,"
replied Asara, almost with a smile,
"if, and only if, you now can say
our love is qualified and less than absolute."

At this, Tol looked out of the window and
then said, "You do not know what things have passed
between Attendant Ito and myself,
resulting in my wearing of this ring.
You do not know what words, before the Lords,
were left unsaid, nor do you know what love

has been expressed, nor that I parted from
her famous beauty, not yours, with a kiss."

Inhaling deeply, Asara wheeled, taking
in her hands a massive ancient door
of stone-hard wood. Its hinges yielded loudly
to her Tersai strength; and with more noise,
her fingers crushed the board in moments to
a soft and fibrous pulp, which she then laid
upon the floor to make a sudden bed.

"Take comfort in my arms," she said to Tol,
"and let me know that you, in making love,
must fail, with your firm body no less than
with words, to hide your love for me. Now roam
the landscape thus revealed as I remove
my clothes, and in my forests and my fields
now build slow structures of sensation, and,
when you complete and dwell in your estate,
let's climb to see the garden tower's view."

The seconds which elapsed, before he moved,
intensified their dance of love with
urgency that scattered shreds of ancient wood
throughout the dusty floor. Later, when echoes
of their union ceased to jar the empty
halls of Station K, caresses gave way
first to wordlessness, next to a long
and glad embrace and, finally, to sleep.

Awaking first, Tol wiped the dust from glowing
screens which told him time was short and that

he soon must go. Asara woke and said:
"When you lived life in our frigid south,
you saw the lower species live and die.
You saw the fingers of pure agony
destroy—by hunger, pestilence, disease—
their short and wretched lives. You heard their cries;
and though you never have felt any pain,
you have imagination such to know
their misery. If you must die by new
infection which envelops Sector Five,
then go. But nothing says you must endure
that pain. Why not pre-set the transport crystals,
and, before you dream their sleep, dispel
this station's atmosphere so that you have
no air? Without it, you shall enter stasis,
losing consciousness before the starbeam's
spark; and like the remnant of dear Olsta
when we came to Attatrul, you shall
not breathe except by application of
some Craft. Since there is no one left in
Sector Five to make you breathe again, you shall,
for all of time, not think one further thought;
and if, by chance, the plague is of such
virulence that it can pierce a Being without
breath, then your unconsciousness is made
quite permanent in that way just as well."

"'By chance,' you say," replied Tol, looking with
impatience at her eyes. "What chance ought I

to take that your suggestion might frustrate
my mission? Ending now the plague, apparently
upon the dictate of the Source,
is reason for my death. It may well be
that this result comes only from my pain
in dying, as a punishment for breach
of our law. My death must have its meaning.
I will not step into that endless night
unless I am quite sure of its result."

"Your answer is the point I wish to make,"
Asara said. "If meaning lies in what
we think will bring results, we must do all
we can and leave no thing to chance. As partner
in your plan to seek the Source, the future
of all space requires that I go.
How can you die if you live on in me?"

With one hand, Tol held hers. With another,
he slid his fingers through her hair. He said,
"Come follow me, and let's look at the stars."
She smiled and followed to the glass. Once there,
they focused on immensity beyond,
as Tol continued in a gentle tone,
"From here, this window dulls our view, as does
the prospect of our death. Yet loving you
makes clarity beyond where eyes may see;
and in your arms and with the memory
of what we've shared, I sense the fullness of
the life that will not be. To sense it, is

to live it in advance; and having loved
you thus through all unending time, our death
together seals, and does not end, our love."

Thus they resolved to meet the end of life
and journey to their fate in Sector Five.
They hugged each other close and did so for
so long a time they did not see, before
they left with hands held tight, an unexpected
stir of lights flick through the starbeam cells.

The Throne

Chapter 10

The Throne

Transmissions pulsed from Centra throughout
space: the Source had spoken but would speak
no more. Authority and origin of law
resided where established by the Source—
All hail to Ito! Ito rules all space!

When Tol had gone one-seventh of the distance
to his death, the Monarch Ito had
made firm her throne. In the millennia
of Centrayears that marked the early days
of Ito's reign, the Overlords gave careful
thought to all that had transpired. Traditions
of the governance of space met swift
collapse, as all the Lords, of all the Higher
Species, faced as fact the silence of
the Source and the finality of all

of Ito's words. Then, on one day when
many mists had cleared and riverbeds baked hard
beneath the staring of Kolku, the Lords
at Centra ended years of wearisome
debate. With only several Kowd in firm
dissent, the Lords resolved, effective from
that day, to terminate their office and
disband the Council of the Overlords.

Not moments after Kowd Uskeete pronounced
the final dissolution of the Lords,
the doors of that great hall swung wide, admitting
shafts of sunlight and a furnace of
dry air. In strode the Monarch Ito, making
gestures to Ra Thon, who, by new custom,
spoke for Ito all her public words.

"All Overlords of Space," she said, "which until
just this moment you have been, rejoin
yourselves, at my command, as council to
myself." The Monarch's Council thus had life;
and it began, on that dry day, to learn
its service of her solitary rule.

News of these things, in an expanding sphere,
grew, at the pace of light from Centran seeds,
to feed the mouth of history of space.

When Tol had gone two-sevenths of the distance
to his death, the Monarch Ito had
completely vanquished truth. Her victory
took place when Bal and Olsta challenged her,

in private audience, that she had spoken
falsehood when she told the Lords that Tol,
by Craft, had made the Envoys think that Bal
was chosen by the Wise of Silver Streams.

The monarch promised them to satisfy
all space, lest any have concern about
her taking power. She invited them,
together with I La and strong Valkav,
the lucky Tersai who had struck the silver
planet's moon, to witness declarations
which, as monarch, she would give to serve
this need. Her speech took place at daybreak on
an open field of grass, an hour's walking
from the City of the Source. There, with
a countless number listening at her feet,
even the birds grew quiet as she spoke.

"All Higher Beings," Ito then began,
with Ra Thon speaking for her all her words,
"both here and throughout space, give heed to learn
how future turns to fact. On worlds in space
that pre-existed those we Higher Species
made, one finds disorder and a
randomness in substance and in form. Deep in
their dirt and rock are places packed with
unused carbon, which by pressure yields up
crystal diamond rock. Our padors chip away
at this so as to find the perfect gem.

"How life will be in future time is like
that diamond rock. First, it is hidden. Then,
when found, it finds perfection, not by something
made, but by removal of what shields
its perfect face. Just so, emergence of
my monarchy required casting off
what would impede its greatness: namely, threats
of certain death. The cuttings from this gem
included one whole world, as well as those
who died in Sector Five, and also Tol,
who has been sent to seal the end of death.

"There is still more to this similitude.
There is still imperfection which prevents
the mounting of this gem to make a jewel.
There are still Higher Beings whose internal
vision is impaired, so that they fail
to see the excellence of what has come
to pass. Behold! Before your eyes stand four
of these defectives: Bal, Olsta, I La,
Valkav. Behold! They shall impede no more!"

A group of padors seized the four and marched
them through the roads and streets and set them on
a starbeam which, on Ito's order, was
directed to no world and aimed towards
a hole in space, wherein was endless sleep.

News of these things, in an expanding sphere,
grew, at the pace of light from Centran seeds,
to feed the mouth of history of space.

When Tol had gone three-sevenths of the distance to his death, the Monarch Ito had confirmed her single power. El, the Kowd among her council who was sponsor of the Great Petition of All Time, made challenge of her having said that the Petition was allowed. To this, she made no answer right away. Instead, she made a firm decree that all who lived on Centra should evacuate, withdrawing by compacted starbeams to an asteroid that shared the lazy Centran orbit of Kolku.

The asteroid had seen no life since battles in the Age of Endless Wars. Its ancient prisons now became the campsite for the whole of Centran life. Ra Thon stood silhouetted as a smoky dawn crept over that small world. She spoke for Ito, who, in glowing robes of green and gold, looked on.

"I serve you as your monarch, and my service lies in bearing all the weight of total power. I, as autocrat, serve more in my restraint than through what I, as just one Being, do. The concentration of such force gives focus to all Higher Beings throughout space; and every thought and act must, in its cause, derive from only me. Before I grant to you the end of change,

I must make sure you understand my role.
Now see the proof of power which I hold."

The planet Centra was, just then, emerging
from the asteroid's horizon. Ito
stretched her pointing finger from the folds
of her bright robe; and when it was in line
with what had been the fulcrum of all life,
then planet Centra, in the silence of
deep space, exploded into fire; and
before the faces of all those who called
it home, the mystic planet ceased to be.

Artists, summoned from nearby, soon replaced
by Craft that world with what was to be called,
by monarchial command, Planet Ita.

News of these things, in an expanding sphere,
grew, at the pace of light from Itan seeds,
to feed the mouth of history of space.

When Tol had gone four-sevenths of the distance
to his death, the Monarch Ito had
set systems in her rule. Her council asked
how Higher Beings might direct themselves
to walk in Ito's paths; and she gave them,
imprinted on a single page, her laws.

"No Being shall," the document began,
"hold title, office, honor or degree
unless it be, directly or by chain
of delegation, from myself. All my
commands are law and shall apply, not only

to their stated ends, but also where,
by clear analogy, they may pertain.
No plan is policy unless conforming
to such principles I state; and you
should formulate requests of me with care,
for I shall give my time but sparingly
to this, issuing edicts but one time
each year. In making, judging and enforcing
of all laws, I am the fountain of
their being and the end of all appeals."

News of these things, in an expanding sphere,
grew, at the pace of light from Itan seeds,
to feed the mouth of history of space.

When Tol had gone five-sevenths of the distance
to his death, the Monarch Ito had
established how all space should make reflection
of her rule. That she had served the Source,
that this same Oracle had made her Lord
of space, that she had brought deliverance from
the plague and stayed alive to rule—all this
betokened tribute. All of space must make
repayment for the gift of Ito's rule.
Ra Thon announced what each must freely give.

"All planets, throughout space, must bend the
hand of art to tribute for our Monarch and
our Lord. By word and picture, hologram
and song, the glorious transition to

her rule must find exalted re-creation
in all sensory effect. When this
transition is complete, and all its
narrative secure, the tribute of each world
shall turn to meditation on what cannot
ever change: sublime and perfect
permanence of Monarch Ito's rule. Fitting
is this tribute, as Ito rules all space!"

News of these things, in an expanding sphere,
grew, at the pace of light from Itan seeds,
to feed the mouth of history of space.

When Tol had gone six-sevenths of the distance
to his death, the Monarch Ito had
built up a monument in which her
person would reside. By her direction,
architects convened to where, on Planet
Ita, canyons through high mountains met beneath
the slopes of one still higher peak. For ten
centuries, teams of padors made a
formal and deliberate procession, through
the canyon floors, each bearing massive
chiselled blocks of onyx, smoky granite and
of jade. The frame was cast in colored
metals, standing outside of the stone. Its name
was Temple Palace; and, soon after its
completion, witnesses filled every
canyon for the solemn hearing of Ra Thon.

"This house is that of Ito, Monarch of
all space. It is wonderful, and superb.
Behold, you planets, greatness, and aspire!"

News of these things, in an expanding sphere,
grew, at the pace of light from Itan seeds,
to feed the mouth of history of space.

When time had fully passed, and Tol had
travelled to his death, the Monarch Ito had
ordained her permanence in power.
All members of her council, grouped within
their Council Hall, made no applause when, at
this time, the terse command from Temple
Palace came: "Tol has arrived and put an end
to death. At your petition now, I grant
the final end to change, as I now rule all space."

The Dream

Chapter 11

The Dream

Consciousness, born of being and of time,
without a past, nor knowledge of itself,
nor any name, moved through sequential
intersections, found in space, of various
dimensions. These events, as points of shared
dimensions might be called, made their direction
through the neutron shield to Sector Five.
Without awareness, it of else, or else
of it, except emerging knowledge that
it newly lived, this consciousness arrived
at one place, not having left another.

It lived—and came to Planet Mergo within
Sector Five. It thought, and its first thought
was of the number 2, enabling
perception of some thing, then things, beyond

itself, although not knowing if, thus
perceiving, it found or made the universe.

Soft falling rains had ceased their rushing
whispers through the land. Among the hills,
around the grassy clearing where the starbeam
crystals lay, small beads of water glistened
briefly, on the fronds of bending plants,
then vanished airborne to the Mergan sun.
No breezes moved the ancient shaded webs
that spiders spun beneath the crystal cups;
and nothing that day moved the faces of
those several Higher Beings standing
vigilant, around, where expectation and
new consciousness required that they be.

They waited for the light to end its dance,
reforming, into substance, Beings whom they knew
to be Asara and her mate. Smiles stole
across the faces of the Tersai and
the Humans when they saw the new arrivals'
clear surprise that any were alive.
The Kowd could sense what they were blind to see.

"You seem to follow me each place I go,"
announced the Kowd Parinmawada,
doubling, by its presence, their surprise.
"Yet, where I welcomed Tol, on Attatrul,
to new concerns and horrors from our past,
I now include Asara in a welcome
to the future of all space. Come, take

delight, and rest; and while this planet loops
its course around a pleasant sun, you shall
know days of unimagined joy and learn
what hidden locks now yield to hidden rooms."

Tol and Asara gingerly emerged
from crystal forms which had received their sleeping
selves. They turned; they stretched; and when they felt
quite certain that they did no longer dream,
Asara smoothed her hair, then yawned and spoke.

"I barely trust my senses that you seem
to live. We came, myself and Tol, expecting
to find death and then to join its ranks.
Instead, we meet pastoral mirth and this
dear Kowd, our friend, we thought we left behind."

The Kowd and others smiled again and brought
the two arrivals to some cottages
nearby, in one of which they bathed and dined
and easily could see this was no world
of death. Around the embers of a
dying flame, beneath the pulsing nighttime
Mergan sky, Parinmawada spoke these words:

"Cast off all perplexity, you who think
to die but find you shall now live. Accept
the very gift of life which you, by coming
here, thought that you would give. Hear now
how history, its mainspring turned too tight,
is now unwinding new directions out
of time. The Leaves of Love I ate at Centra

had evolved to something new. They brought
me what the Mergan pilgrims were the first
to share: the sphere of common thought.
By this, myself and all who have consumed
those leaves share consciousness that has no bound
in time or space. By this, our minds refer
to thinking vastly greater than our own;
and access to this consciousness gives us,
when needed, insight from perspectives outside
time. By this, I knew I should come here."

"By this, as well," intoned Kuurstat, the Planet
Mergo's Tersai Lord and artist famous for
her watercolor brush, "we can interpret
fact. The part of our consciousness
we share permits us to infer the meaning
and the progress of events. For instance,
after eating from the Centratrees
and then returning home, we found ourselves
discussing news, from Centra, but which never
had arrived. Inferences did not
need fact, and talk of this did not need speech.

"We knew, from nowhere, that the Overlords
had made petition to abolish future
change. We comprehended, in one thought,
the emptiness of such stagnation and
our role to intervene. In common thought,
the future had arrived before the past
was gone; for by this mode, unbuffered by

the lightspeed bar of space, we saw, and shared,
the origin and ending of the Source.
Great Universal Source! Arisen in
mystery, dwelling at Enigma, gone
with no more reason than for when it came."

"The answer strangely lay with us, the Kowd,"
Parinmawada interrupted then
Kuurstat. "We now perceive that in our
meditation through the years we have, without
our knowing, generated thoughts the force
of which combined to be the Source. By eating
of the Leaves of Love, when time had ripened
them to this new taste, the Mergan Beings
were the first to share—and do so
consciously—this general meditation of
the Kowd. The flame that was the Source now
flickers, dimly, within sight of common thought."

"And we saw," said Kuurstat, continuing,
"as after our pilgrimage we could,
that history advances by the knowledge
it must teach, that all of space must learn
it must evolve, that Higher Beings must
endure the seeming end of change, and that
the treachery of politics, long buried
in our past, would serve to show what powers
of confinement must prevail in life
that does not change. We fashioned such deceit
as would bring this to pass: first, sending signals

that a plague tore through our worlds, second,
focusing common thought so that the Source,
which common thought had joined and had become...."

"But which the Mergan Kowd then realized
their meditations had been forming throughout
time," Parinmawada pointed out.

"Quite so," Kuurstat went on, "but as I say,
we focused thought to send oracular
direction to Attendant Ito,
isolating her to be the instrument to grant
the Overlords' request to end all change."

"And you assaulted her great soul," said Tol,
"beating down her will, twisting it to serve
your terror of untruth. She has become,
by this your fraud, as I have learned that word,
an undeserving victim, charged by you
to victimize all space and terminate
the beauty of my world. Justify this."

"Do not imagine, Tol," Parinmawada
said, "that we, who have consumed the leaves,
have made a substitution of the Source
with our will. We consciously participate,
but do not have control, in common thought.
When you partake, yourself, of these new leaves,
you shall perceive your role to act—but not
to write—the drama that is history
in space. How we, the Higher Species, may

in future learn of error, without
demonstration it is so, is future thought."

"Consider too how we have oiled this
transition to new life," then spoke Kuurstat.
"As we were privy to pronouncements, first
to Ito, then yourself, we knew your world
would end. We sent some of ourselves, by starbeams
to the planets near that sphere, who rescued,
by the simplest Craft, all Beings from
your world when it disjoined—except, of course,
Asara, Olsta and your friend, Valkav,
all three of whom still had more roles to play.
All others from the world of silver streams
now dwell with us on Mergo and nearby.
We also plucked I La, Bal, Olsta and Valkav
from paths to endless sleep, although
of this, and of a special harvest brought
from Centran soil, you both have yet to learn."

"What need I further know, for now and for
all time?" Asara asked in nearly weeping
joy. "My people were forever lost,
dispersed, with only traces then entrusted
to imperfect memory. All thanks
to your great love, my planet has resphered."

Tol reflected, brooding, and then he spoke.
"May relief such as this, that death does not
now live, etch, throughout space, the memory
of every Higher Being, such that so

unequalled agony of deep concern
may fix in all of us the lesson of these days.
My friend, Parinmawada, tell me, though,
what might prevent what happened once before,
when, at the abolition of all death,
all memory, of what had been, was lost."

"Know one thing more," the Kowd replied, "by
joining knowledge of a present state of time,
I could, as I explained to you, infer
some features of the past. In further
contemplation, I discerned that, after Higher
Beings first converged in space, their stark resolve
to kill each other far outlived their lives.
For generations, they made war; and to
this life of death, replacement beings, known
as children, were all born. They heeded common
purpose only when, by lapse of time,
all matter cooled and all the universe
collapsed into a shrinking spiral which,
they soon perceived, would force retreat
beyond the last horizon of events,
a singularity, where all prediction fails
and where there is no time, no space, no life.

"Facing their common end, where all effects
must reach at last their cause, they ceased to fight.
They marshalled forces which today we know
as Craft. They made adjustment to their ending
which, they thought correctly, might begin

again. Thus, by the efforts of those drained
to formlessness, all Higher Beings knew
no death when they were re-created and,
with all existence, lived again in time.
So memory had ceased, when time had ceased,
and was no more when time again resumed.
Your answer, Tol, lies in the question of
what Craft we next can funnel outside time."

Hearing this, Tol embraced Asara in
his arms, and he and she soon took their leave
from all their smiling hosts. For several days,
they kept apart and found, in sweet inactive time,
relief and happy comfort by themselves.

It was, on Mergo, harvest at that time.
The weary padors cut, and stored, the fruit
of fertile ground; and all throughout that world,
its feasts and ancient dances filled the air
with smells and sounds of joy. Tol and Asara
shared this time, in sweet reunion, with
the people of their world of silver streams.

"Now is the time," announced Kuurstat, when
harvesting was done, "that our guests, from
unenlightened space, should see through windows
opened by the leaves on Centra grown, learning
the outside of the cabin of their minds.

"I once could trust no fact or thing," said Tol,
receiving in his hands the crumbling blooms,
"but now I hold in what I hold all trust."

He and Asara ate; and what appeared
to others as a momentary pause
unfolded slowly, to their inner selves,
a common dream whose textures mixed rich colors
with a blur of time and touch and taste
and sound. In this wide dream, the Aliadni
memories, though long since stilled in Tol,
came plodding to a darkened stage and played
three acts, in which Tol and Asara seemed
as one, one actor for whom this was real.

First, darkness yielded to the daylight screams
of birth, and in one moment they felt pain
of being born and that of giving life.
Relief and outrage mingled and then yielded
to the acquiescing fact of drawing
routine breath, and all was calm again.

The second phase was longer than the first.
It spun around them nets and strings and ropes
that were their parents, children, spouses, friends,
their secret lovers, allies, teachers, slaves,
their benefactors, known and unknown, and,
at last, themselves. By these, they sought, but could
not reach, safety, so dimly seen beyond
the urgent waters of their sickness, pain
and hunger—and their desperate need to breathe.

The final panel fused, in smoking union,
sudden apprehension and a longing
for the end. The universe and all

its worth receded through the haze, leaving
an absence, void even of vacuum, blank
as pools of water where no wind has breathed.
    The dream was over, and they wept to live again.

The Celebration

Chapter 12

The Celebration

"I have had news that will stir all to joy,"
the Planetlord of Attatrul announced.
All citizens within Bandoo, and many
from afar, had come to stand in noonday
heat to hear what Ilka had to say.
"I only wish my powers could conceal,"
she smiling said, "the busy labors of
my padors, in these past few days, to make
now ready feast and dance. Prepare yourselves,
my fellow Beings of this wooden world,
to hear what novel thing, of which I am
myself yet unaware, dwells at the core
of recent Itan edicts to rejoice."

Skilful horns, in tight harmony, disturbed
the air; and vague but visible

uneasiness appeared among the crowd. A scroll,
which starbeams had that morning yielded up
to waiting hands, flashed its bright whiteness as
the planetlord extended it and read.

"Hear this of Ito, ruler sole of all
that is: 'Good Universe—for which I made
my throne, purged imperfection, founded Ita,
wrote my laws, established tribute, and
at last, confirmed my temple—be now
gratified that these good works are now forever
sealed, for benefit of all, by my granting
the petition, which abolishes all change,
and by my now announcing this is so.'

"This news," said Ilka to her world, "has borne
its fruit, at lightspeed, throughout space;
and having reached its limit here, its final
flower brings, with it, great cause to make
a celebration of its bloom. Each planet,
as these tidings made their way, was told
to mark the time when, by our learning, space
was made complete. All Higher Beings have,
then, waited for this day; and we shall eat
and dance, this eve, in happy knowledge that
all space rejoices with us at this time."

No horns dispersed the crowd, which left to
dress in evening garb. The padors, meanwhile, made
their distribution of the special food
which had, by starbeam, made appearance after

Ito's scroll. This seeming gift bore strict instruction, on each leafy bale, that every Higher Being taste of it that day.

Sunset came and triggered festive lights. The wooden streets lay quiet, beneath careful festoonery, until the sanctioned noise.

Rows and columns of musicians marched. Into the evening, into the dusk, in brisk parade, the uniforms paced. Step sounded with step. Note sounded with note. Throughout Bandoo, throughout that world, across the universe, strict to the orders of synchronous march, celebrants made their joyous trek.

The air was cool and still when Ilka stood to speak, before her banquet hall and on the telescreens of halls throughout her world.

"It might not be my choice," she said, "if my impulsiveness and quest for pleasure were entrusted so to choose, to cast our future days from one unchanging mold. Why should I be, forever, planetlord to you...."

The crowd awakened at those words and stopped her with their loud protesting that her world was hers—and still most loyal to her rule.

"How good, for you, you want no change," replied their Planetlord, with wistful resignation and, some thought, a trace of sad dismay. "Perhaps," said Ilka, "now I shall take time

to learn how many spouses I have wed.
Appreciation, not new conquest, shall
be my ambition, from now on, in love.
But now, to celebrate. Lift up your glasses.
Drink and eat, and, with the rest of space,
just at this moment, welcome future joy."

And thus it was, whether for the first time
or the second, all Higher Beings tasted
Leaves of Love, so carefully engrafted
by the Mergan Beings onto Ito's
plans. The rush of common thought came like
a springtime sluice, washing opaqueness from
a window view of all the planets, all
the stars, and all immensity of space
and time. With all inhabitants as witness,
curving bars of color, or, perhaps,
of sound, imposed a bright connecting mesh
which joined each place, where Higher Beings dwelled,
making known that each now shared the feel
and taste and smell of this panoptic field.

The first shared thought was wonderment, and
questioning, by what new Craft the Higher Species
could, across all space and with no words,
think as one mind and know that they so did,
each one a part, yet separate from all.

Then came understanding and explanations
from Sector Five. From there, the sphere of long
habituated common thought, among those

long thought dead, merged with the rest of space.
Narrative, viewed from outside time, revealed
in its cross sections what foundations of
experience must serve all future time.

The winds of these sensations soon abated
to real time; and like so many dazed
and speechless planetlords throughout the reach
of space, the lord called Ilka glared through eyes
transfixed in swelling puzzlement and awe.

"I might now dare conclude," she spoke, as she
began to focus on the crowds beneath
her feet, "that we have more to celebrate
than first we might have thought. Thinking,
unbound by space or time, has stripped ten thousand
centuries of great illusion, and
of misdirection, so that now we all...."

"The Kowd! The Kowd!" a panicked cry burst
upwards from the multitude. Everywhere
in sight, all Kowd lay motionless and on
examination proved to be quite dead.
The urgent voices of the crowd increased
in pitch. Many Beings began to run.

"Some new deception has unloosed the plague,
and now we all shall die!" one voice eclipsed
the rest. Fear, never felt before on
Attatrul, now freely twisted through the
pathways of their minds, finding no remedy.

They scattered past the padors, who began
to stop them and to speak to them in words
far past the understanding of their kind.

"I live, but in another flesh!" said one.

"I apprehend the shape of distant things!"
another spoke, while gazing with unblinking
eyes upon the colored banners on
the wall. The other padors, too, spoke up.

"I have control of arms and legs, and thus
I move myself and other things," observed
one pador, picking up an empty chair.

Confusion came and just as quickly went
as common thought, again, united all
their minds, this time emitting words that were
the overlap between the common sphere
and all the meditations of one Kowd,
Parinmawada; and those words were these:

"There now can be no end of change, nor, even
less, beginning of predicting of
our fate. We Kowd among us have assumed,
by forces beyond Craft, the living
carcasses of padors who once served; and they,
all of us, now partake of sight, of movement,
and of extreme arbitrariness
in our assignment to a sex. I sense
already, as a seeing female, that
my thought shall be distracted from the

meditation, which, for all us Kowd, was all
there was to life, within the darkened mind.
"All Beings know, by joining to the common
thought—which, from the Source, takes governance
of space—the story of Asara's love,
of Tol's great quest, and Ito's great deceit.
We know release from lies which built a prison
outward from the Temple Palace walls.
Let us, renewed, return to work too long
declined; let us make history in space;
and let us now make firm our base, and tell,
by joining all its tellers to one tale,
the three-fold narrative, which made us whole.
"Here is a story which, by being told,
ensures that its events may keep their force,
in face of all the limits, or the
boundlessness, of space, or any flux of time.
Give thought in common on that day when it
began, a point of time and space condensed
beyond all measure, all still to unfold...."

About the Author

Born in 1955, in Drexel Hill, Pennsylvania, J. Gardner Hodder is a graduate of St. Paul's School, Concord, New Hampshire. He holds degrees from Harvard, the University of Pennsylvania and the University of Toronto.

Formerly a journalist based in St. John's, Newfoundland, he has lived since 1980 in Toronto, where he practices law and writes. In Canada, his writing has appeared in such publications as *The Globe and Mail*, *The Evening Telegram*, *Atlantic Insight*, and *The Financial Times*.

He lives with his wife, Elizabeth Harvey, and their son, Matthew.